CliffsNotes™

Atlas Shrugged

By Andrew Bernstein, Ph.D.

IN THIS BOOK

- Learn about the life and philosophy of Ayn Rand
- Preview an introduction to *Atlas Shrugged*
- Explore the novel's themes and character development in the Critical Commentaries
- Examine in-depth Character Analyses
- Acquire an understanding of key themes with Critical Essays
- Reinforce what you learn with the CliffsNotes Review
- Find additional information to further your study in the CliffsNotes Resource Center and online at www.cliffsnotes.com

WILEY

Wiley Publishing, Inc.

About the Author

Andrew Bernstein holds a Ph.D. in Philosophy from the Graduate School of the City University of New York. He teaches Philosophy at Pace University in Pleasantville, New York, and at the State University of New York at Purchase. Dr. Bernstein is a speaker for the Ayn Rand Institute and lectures on Ayn Rand's novels throughout the United States.

Publisher's Acknowledgments

Editorial

Project Editor: Joan Friedman
Copy Editor: Billie A. Williams
Acquisitions Editor: Gregory W. Tubach
Glossary Editors: The editors and staff of Webster's New World Dictionaries
Editorial Administrator: Michelle Hacker

Composition

Indexer: York Production Services, Inc.
Proofreader: York Production Services, Inc.

Wiley Indianapolis Composition Services

CliffsNotes™ *Atlas Shrugged*

Published by:
Wiley Publishing, Inc.
111 River Street
Hoboken, NJ 07030
www.wiley.com

Table of Contents

How to Use This Book

This CliffsNotes study guide on Rand's *Atlas Shrugged* supplements the original literary work, giving you background information about the author, an introduction to the work, a graphical character map, critical commentaries, expanded glossaries, and a comprehensive index, all for you to use as an educational tool that will allow you to better understand *Atlas Shrugged*. This study guide was written with the assumption that you have read *Atlas Shrugged*. Reading a literary work doesn't mean that you immediately grasp the major themes and devices used by the author; this study guide will help supplement your reading to be sure you get all you can from Rand's *Atlas Shrugged*. CliffsNotes Review tests your comprehension of the original text and reinforces learning with questions and answers, practice projects, and more. For further information on Ayn Rand and *Atlas Shrugged*, check out the CliffsNotes Resource Center..

CliffsNotes provides the following icons to highlight essential elements of particular interest:

Reveals the underlying themes in the work.

Helps you to more easily relate to or discover the depth of a character.

Uncovers elements such as setting, atmosphere, mystery, passion, violence, irony, symbolism, tragedy, foreshadowing, and satire.

Enables you to appreciate the nuances of words and phrases.

Don't Miss Our Web Site

Discover classic literature as well as modern-day treasures by visiting the CliffsNotes Web site at www.cliffsnotes.com. You can obtain a quick download of a CliffsNotes title, purchase a title in print form, browse our catalog, or view online samples.

You'll also find interactive tools that are fun and informative, links to interesting Web sites, tips, articles, and additional resources to help you, not only for literature, but for test prep, finance, careers, computers, and the Internet too. See you at www.cliffsnotes.com!

LIFE AND BACKGROUND OF THE AUTHOR

The following abbreviated biography of Ayn Rand is provided so that you might become more familiar with her life and the historical times that possibly influenced her writing. Read this Life and Background of the Author section and recall it when reading Rand's *Atlas Shrugged*, thinking of any thematic relationship between Rand's work and his life.

Personal Background

Ayn Rand was born Alissa Rosenbaum in 1905 in St. Petersburg, Russia. Rand was raised in an upper-middle-class, European-oriented family, in the midst of the mysticism and nationalism of Russia. Having taught herself to read, Rand, at the age of 8, became captivated by the heroism in a French-language serial adventure entitled *The Mysterious Valley*. At the age of 9, Rand decided to become a writer, inspired especially by Victor Hugo's novels. Hugo's writing helped arm her against the fatalistic view of life that dominated Russia, a country she later described as "an accidental cesspool of civilization."

Education and Early Life

In February of 1917, Ayn Rand witnessed the first shots of the Russian Revolution, and later that year she witnessed the Bolshevik Revolution as well. In order to escape the fighting, her family went to the Crimea, where Rand finished high school. The final Communist victory brought the confiscation of her father's pharmacy and periods of near-starvation. When introduced to American history in her last year of high school, Rand immediately took America as her model of what a nation of free men could be. Her love for the West—especially America—was fueled by Viennese operettas and American and German films, which the Soviets temporarily allowed to be shown.

When Rand and her family returned from the Crimea, she entered the University of Petrograd to study philosophy and history, graduating in 1924. She entered the State Institute for Cinema Arts in 1924 to study screenwriting. During this period, Rand produced her first formal writings, essays about Hollywood, published in 1999 by The Ayn Rand Institute Press as *Russian Writings on Hollywood*.

Immigration to the United States

In late 1925, Ayn Rand obtained permission to leave the Soviet Union to visit relatives in the United States, on the pretext of learning the American film business. After six months with relatives in Chicago, she moved to Hollywood to pursue a career as a screenwriter. On her second day there, she had a chance meeting with her favorite American director, Cecil B. DeMille, who took her to the set of his epic film *The King of Kings* and gave her a job, first as an extra, then as a script reader.

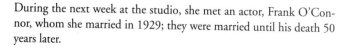

During the next week at the studio, she met an actor, Frank O'Connor, whom she married in 1929; they were married until his death 50 years later.

Career Highlights

After struggling for several years at various non-writing jobs, including one in the wardrobe department at the RKO film studio, Rand sold her first screenplay, *Red Pawn*, to Universal Studios in 1932. Rand saw her first stage play, *Night of January 16th*, produced in Hollywood in 1934 and then on Broadway in 1935. Her first novel, *We the Living*, was completed in 1933. The most autobiographical of Rand's novels, *We the Living*, was rejected as too anti-Communist and wasn't published in the United States until 1936. In 1937, Rand devoted a few weeks to writing her novella *Anthem*, which was soon published in England but not published in the United States until 1947.

Although positively reviewed, neither *We the Living* nor *Anthem* garnered high sales. Not until the publication of *The Fountainhead* did Ayn Rand achieve fame. Rand began writing *The Fountainhead* in 1935, taking seven years to complete the book. In the character of architect Howard Roark, she presented for the first time the kind of hero whose depiction was the chief goal of her writing: the ideal man, man "as he could be and ought to be." *The Fountainhead* was rejected by 12 publishers but finally accepted by Bobbs-Merrill. Although published in 1943, *The Fountainhead* made history by becoming a best-seller two years later, through word-of-mouth, and it gained for its author lasting recognition as a champion of individualism.

Ayn Rand returned to Hollywood in late 1943 to write the screenplay for *The Fountainhead*, but war-time restrictions delayed production until 1948. Working part-time as a screenwriter for producer Hal Wallis, Rand wrote such scripts as *Love Letters* and *You Came Along* and began *Atlas Shrugged* in 1946. In 1951, Rand moved permanently back to New York City and devoted herself full-time to the completion of *Atlas Shrugged*, which was published in 1957. Despite extremely negative reviews, *Atlas Shrugged* quickly became a best-seller.

Rand's Philosophy: Objectivism

After the publication of *Atlas Shrugged*, Ayn Rand realized that she would have to identify the philosophy that made her heroes possible.

She termed it Objectivism and described it as "a philosophy for living on earth." Rand's theory holds that man gains knowledge only through reason. The "Objectivism in Action" section of the Introduction to the Novel offers further insight into Rand's belief system.

Rand offered private courses on both fiction and nonfiction writing and, in 1958, helped start an institute that teaches her philosophy. For the remaining years of her life, Rand devoted herself to nonfiction writing, penning, and editing a number of articles for her periodicals. These articles later appeared in numerous philosophic collections and dealt with topics including ethics (*The Virtue of Selfishness*), politics (*Capitalism: the Unknown Ideal*), aesthetics (*The Romantic Manifesto*), and the theory of knowledge (*Introduction to Objectivist Epistemology*). At the time of her death in 1982, Rand was working on a television miniseries of *Atlas Shrugged*.

A controversial novelist and philosopher—especially in academic circles—Ayn Rand attained widespread recognition, as indicated by a 1991 joint survey by The Library of Congress and The Book of the Month Club, which placed *Atlas Shrugged* second only to the Bible as the most influential book among American readers. Signs of her influence began to blossom in the mid-1980s and accelerated throughout the 1990s. In 1985, the Ayn Rand Institute in Marina del Rey, California, was established to increase the awareness of the existence and content of Ayn Rand's philosophy. Also in the mid-1980s, the Ayn Rand Society—an organization of professional philosophers devoted to studying and teaching her theories—was founded within the American Philosophical Association. A steady stream of books analyzing Objectivism has been published in recent years, and in 1995, *The New York Times* started reviewing those books. In 1997, a documentary film devoted to her life (*Ayn Rand: A Sense of Life*) was nominated for an Academy Award. In 1999, the U.S. Postal Service issued a first-class stamp commemorating her achievements.

Ayn Rand's ideas—and *Atlas Shrugged*, her greatest book and primary means of communicating those ideas—are an enduring part of American intellectual culture.

INTRODUCTION TO THE NOVEL

The following Introduction section is provided solely as an educational tool and is not meant to replace the experience of your reading the work. Read the Introduction and A Brief Synopsis to enhance your understanding of the work and to prepare yourself for the critical thinking that should take place whenever you read any work of fiction or nonfiction. Keep the List of Characters and Character Map at hand so that as you read the original literary work, if you encounter a character about whom you're uncertain, you can refer to the List of Characters and Character Map to refresh your memory

Introduction

Atlas Shrugged is Ayn Rand's masterpiece and the culmination of her career as a novelist. With its publication in 1957, the author accomplished everything she wanted to in the realm of fiction; the rest of her career as a writer was devoted to nonfiction. Rand was already a famous, best-selling author by the time she published *Atlas Shrugged*. With the success of *The Fountainhead* a decade earlier and its subsequent production as a Hollywood film starring Gary Cooper in 1949, her stature as an author was established. Publishers knew that her fiction would sell, and consequently they bid for the right to publish her next book.

Atlas Shrugged, although enormously controversial, had no difficulty finding a publisher. On the contrary, Rand conducted an intellectual auction among competing publishers, finally deciding on Random House because its editorial staff had the best understanding of the book. Bennett Cerf was a famous editor there. When Rand explained that, at one level, *Atlas Shrugged* was to provide a moral defense of capitalism, the editorial staff responded, "But that would mean challenging 3,000 years of Judeo-Christian tradition." Their depth of philosophical insight impressed Ayn Rand, and she decided that Random House was the company to publish her book.

Atlas Shrugged furthers the theme of individualism that Ayn Rand developed in *The Fountainhead*. In *The Fountainhead*, she shows by means of its hero, the innovative architect Howard Roark, that the independent mind is responsible for all human progress and prosperity. In *Atlas Shrugged*, she shows that without the independent mind, our society would collapse into primitive savagery. *Atlas Shrugged* is an impassioned defense of the freedom of man's mind. But to understand the author's sense of urgency, we must have an idea of the context in which the book was written. This includes both the post-World War II Cold War and the broader trends of modern intellectual culture.

The Cold War and Collectivism

Twentieth-century culture spawned the most oppressive dictatorships in human history. The Fascists in Italy, the National Socialists (Nazis) in Germany, and the Communists—first in Russia and later in China and elsewhere—seriously threatened individual freedom throughout the world. Ayn Rand lived through the heart of this terrifying historical period. In fact, when she started writing *Atlas Shrugged* in 1946, the West had just achieved victory over the Nazis. For years, the specter of national socialism had haunted the world, exterminating millions of innocent people, enslaving millions more, and threatening the freedom of the entire globe. The triumph of the free countries of the West over Naziism was achieved at an enormous cost in human life. However, it left the threat of communism unabated.

Ayn Rand was born in Russia in 1905 and witnessed firsthand the Bolshevik Revolution, the Communist conquest of Russia, and the political oppression that followed. Even after her escape from the Soviet Union and her safe arrival in the United States, she kept in close touch with family members who remained there. But when the murderous policies of Joseph Stalin swallowed the Soviet Union, she lost track of her family. From her own life experiences, Ayn Rand knew the brutal oppression of Communist tyranny.

During the last days of World War II and in the years immediately following, communism conquered large portions of the world. Soviet armies first rolled through the countries of Eastern Europe, setting up Russian "satellite" nations in East Germany, Poland, Hungary, Romania, and elsewhere. Communists then came to power in China and North Korea and launched an invasion of South Korea. Shortly thereafter, communism was also dominant in Cuba, on America's doorstep. In the 1940s and 1950s, communism was an expanding military power, threatening to engulf the free world.

This time period was the height of the Cold War—the ideological battle between the United States and the Soviet Union. The Soviet Union ruled its empire in Eastern Europe by means of terror, brutally suppressing an uprising by Hungarian freedom fighters in 1956. The Russians developed the atomic bomb and amassed huge armies in Eastern Europe, threatening the free nations of the West. Speaking at the United Nations, Soviet dictator Nikita Khrushchev vowed that communism would "bury" the West. Like the Nazis in the 1930s, communists stood for a *collectivist* political system: one in which an individual is morally obliged to sacrifice himself for the state. Intellectual freedom and individual rights, cherished in the United States and other Western countries, were in grave danger.

Foreign military power was not the only way in which communism threatened U.S. freedom. Collectivism was an increasingly popular political philosophy among American intellectuals and politicians. In the 1930s, both national socialism and communism had supporters among American thinkers, businessmen, politicians, and labor leaders. The full horror of Naziism was revealed during World War II, and support for national socialism dwindled in the United States as a result. But communism, in the form of Marxist political ideology, survived World War II in the United States. Many American professors, writers, journalists, and politicians continued to advocate Marxist principles. When Ayn Rand was writing *Atlas Shrugged,* many Americans strongly believed that the government should have the power to coercively redistribute income and to regulate private industry. The capitalist system of political and economic freedom was consistently attacked by socialists and welfare statists. The belief that an individual has a right to live his own life was replaced, to a significant extent, by the collectivist idea that individuals must work and live in service to other people. Individual rights and political freedom were threatened in American politics, education, and culture.

An Appeal for Freedom

Rand argues in *Atlas Shrugged* that the freedom of American society is responsible for its greatest achievements. For example, in the nineteenth century, inventors and entrepreneurs created an outpouring of innovations that raised the standard of living to unprecedented heights and changed forever the way people live. Rand, who thoroughly researched the history of capitalism, was well aware of the progress made during this period of economic freedom. Samuel Morse invented the telegraph—a device later improved by Thomas Edison, who went on to invent the phonograph, the electric light, and the motion picture projector. John Roebling perfected the suspension bridge and, just before his death, designed his masterpiece, the Brooklyn Bridge. Henry Ford revolutionized the transportation industry by mass-producing automobiles, a revolution that the Wright Brothers carried to the next level with their invention of the airplane. Railroad builders like Cornelius Vanderbilt and James J. Hill established inexpensive modes of transportation and opened up the Pacific Northwest to economic development.

Likewise, Alexander Graham Bell invented the telephone during this era, Cyrus McCormick the reaper, and Elias Howe the sewing machine. Charles Goodyear discovered the vulcanization process that made rubber useful, and George Eastman revolutionized photography with the invention of a new type of camera—the Kodak. George Washington Carver, among myriad agricultural accomplishments, developed peanuts

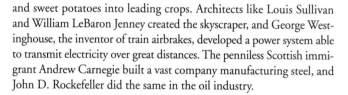

and sweet potatoes into leading crops. Architects like Louis Sullivan and William LeBaron Jenney created the skyscraper, and George Westinghouse, the inventor of train airbrakes, developed a power system able to transmit electricity over great distances. The penniless Scottish immigrant Andrew Carnegie built a vast company manufacturing steel, and John D. Rockefeller did the same in the oil industry.

These are a few examples from an exhaustive list of advances in the late nineteenth and early twentieth centuries. Ayn Rand argues that economic freedom liberated these great creative thinkers, permitting them to put into practice new ideas and methods. But what would happen if economic freedom were lost?

Atlas Shrugged provides Ayn Rand's answer to this question. In the story, she projects the culmination of America's twentieth-century socialist trend. The U.S. government portrayed in the story has significant control over the domestic economy. The rest of the world has been swallowed up by communist "Peoples' States" and subsists in abject poverty. A limited degree of economic freedom still exists in America, but it is steadily declining, as is American prosperity. The successful are heavily taxed to support the poor, and the American poor are similarly levied to finance the even poorer people in foreign Peoples' States. The government subsidizes inefficient businesses at the expense of the more efficient. With the state controlling large portions of the economy, the result is the rise of corrupt businessmen who seek profit by manipulating crooked politicians rather than by doing productive work. The government forces inventors to give up their patents so that all manufacturers may benefit equally from new products. Similarly, the government breaks up productive companies, compelling them to share the market with weaker (less efficient) competitors. In short, the fictionalized universe of *Atlas Shrugged* presents a future in which the U.S. trend toward socialism has been accelerated. Twentieth-century realities such as heavy taxation, massive social welfare programs, tight governmental regulation of industry, and antitrust action against successful companies are heightened in the universe of this story. The government annuls the rights of American citizens, and freedom is steadily eroded. The United States of the novel—the last bastion of liberty on earth— rapidly becomes a fascist/communist dictatorship.

The result, in Rand's fictional universe, is a collapse of American prosperity. Great minds are shackled by government policies, and their innovations are either rejected or expropriated by the state. Thinkers lack the freedom necessary to create new products, to start their own companies, to compete openly, and to earn wealth. Under the increasing yoke of tyranny, the most independent minds in American society choose to defend their liberty in the most effective manner possible: They withdraw from society.

The Mind on Strike

Atlas Shrugged is a novel about a strike. Ayn Rand sets out to show the fate that befalls the world when the thinkers and creators go on strike. The author raises an intriguing question: What would happen if the scientists, medical researchers, inventors, industrialists, writers, artists, and so on withheld their minds and their achievements from the world?

In this novel, Rand argues that all human progress and prosperity depend on rational thinking. For example, human beings have cured such diseases as malaria, polio, dysentery, cholera, diphtheria, and tuberculosis. Man has learned to fly, erect cities and skyscrapers, grow an abundant food supply, and create computers. Humans have been to the moon and back and have invented the telephone, radio, television, and a thousand other life-promoting technologies. All of these achievements result from the human application of a rational mind to practical questions of survival. If the intellectuals responsible for such advances abandon the world, regression to the primitive conditions of the Dark Ages would result. But what would motivate intellectuals to such an extreme act as going on strike? We are used to hearing about strikes that protest conditions considered oppressive or intolerable by workers. The thinkers go on strike in *Atlas Shrugged* to protest the oppression of their intellect and creativity.

The thinkers in *Atlas Shrugged* strike on behalf of individual rights and political freedom. They strike against an enforced moral code of self-sacrifice—the creed that human life must be devoted to serving the needs of others. Above all, the thinkers strike to prove that reason is the only means by which man can understand reality and make proper decisions; emotions should not guide human behavior. In short, the creative minds are on strike in support of a person's right to think and live independently.

In the novel, the withdrawal of the great thinkers causes the collapse of the American economy and the end of dictatorship. The strike proves the role that the rational mind plays in the attainment of progress and prosperity. The emphasis on reason is the hallmark of Ayn Rand's fiction. All of her novels, in one form or another, glorify the life-giving power of the human mind.

For example, in *The Fountainhead*, Ayn Rand emphasizes the independent nature of the mind's functioning—that rational individuals neither conform to society nor obey authority, but trust their own judgment. In her early novelette *Anthem*, Ayn Rand shows that under a collectivist dictatorship, the mind is stifled and society regresses to a condition of primitive ignorance. *Anthem* focuses on the mind's need for political freedom. The focus of *Atlas Shrugged* is the role that the human mind plays in human existence. *Atlas Shrugged* shows that rational thinking is mankind's survival instrument, just as the ability to fly is the survival tool for birds. In all of her major novels, Ayn Rand presents heroes and heroines who are brilliant thinkers opposed to either society's pressure to conform or a dictatorial government's commands to obey. The common denominator in all of her books is the life-and-death importance, for both the individual and society, of remaining true to the mind.

Objectivism in Action

In *Atlas Shrugged*, Ayn Rand presents, for the first time and in a dramatized form, her original philosophy of Objectivism. She exemplifies this philosophy in the lives of the heroes and in the action of the story. *Objectivism* holds that reason—not faith or emotionalism—is man's sole means of gaining knowledge. Her theory states that an individual has a right to his or her own life and to the pursuit of his or her own happiness, which is counter to the view that man should sacrifice himself to God or society. Objectivism is individualistic, holding that the purpose of government is to protect the sovereign rights of an individual. This philosophy opposes the collectivist notion that society as a whole is superior to the individual, who must subordinate himself to its requirements. In the political/economic realm, Objectivism upholds full laissez-faire capitalism—a system of free markets that legally prevent the government from restricting man's productive activities—as the only philosophical system that protects the freedom of man's mind, the rights of the individual, and the prosperity of man's life on earth.

Because of Ayn Rand's uncompromising defense of the mind, of the individual, and of capitalism, *Atlas Shrugged* created great controversy on its publication in 1957. Denounced by critics and intellectuals, the book nevertheless reached a wide audience. The book has sold millions of copies and influenced the lives of countless readers. Since 1957, Ayn Rand's philosophy of Objectivism has gradually taken hold in American society. Today, her books and ideas are becoming widely taught in high schools and universities.

A Brief Synopsis

The story of *Atlas Shrugged* takes place in the United States at an unspecified future time. Dagny Taggart, vice president in charge of operations for Taggart Transcontinental Railroad, seeks to rebuild the crumbling track of the Rio Norte Line that serves Ellis Wyatt's oil fields and the booming industrial areas of Colorado. The country is in a downward economic spiral with businesses closing and men out of work. Other countries in the world have become socialist Peoples' States and are destitute. Colorado, based on Wyatt's innovative method of extracting oil from shale, is the last great industrial center on earth. Dagny intends to provide Colorado the train service it requires, but her brother James Taggart, president of Taggart Transcontinental, tries to block her from getting new rails from Rearden Steel, the last reliable steel manufacturer. James wants to do business with the inefficient Associated Steel, which is run by his friend Orren Boyle. Dagny wants the new rail to be made of Rearden Metal, a new alloy that Hank Rearden developed after ten years of experiment. Because the metal has never been tried and has been denounced by metallurgists, James won't accept responsibility for using it. Dagny, who studied engineering in college, has seen the results of Rearden's tests. She accepts the responsibility and orders the rails made of Rearden Metal.

Worsening the economic depression in the U.S. is the unexplained phenomenon of talented men retiring and disappearing. For example, Owen Kellogg, a bright young Taggart employee for whom Dagny had great hopes, tells her that he is leaving the railroad. McNamara, a contractor who was supposed to rebuild the Rio Norte Line, retires unexpectedly. As more great men disappear, the American people become increasingly pessimistic. Dagny dislikes the new phrase that has crept into the language and signifies people's sense of futility and despair. Nobody knows the origin or exact meaning of the question "Who is John Galt?," but people use the unanswerable question to express their sense of hopelessness. Dagny rejects the widespread pessimism and finds a new contractor for the Rio Norte Line.

The crisis for Taggart Transcontinental worsens when the railroad's San Sebastian Line proves to be worthless and is nationalized by the Mexican government. The line, which cost millions of dollars, was supposed to provide freight service for the San Sebastian Mines, a new venture by Francisco d'Anconia, the wealthiest copper industrialist in the world. Francisco was Dagny's childhood friend and her former lover, but she now regards him as a worthless playboy. In this latest venture, d'Anconia has steered investors completely wrong, causing huge financial losses and a general sense of unrest.

James Taggart, in an attempt to recover the railroad's losses on the San Sebastian Line, uses his political friendships to influence the vote of the National Alliance of Railroads. The Alliance passes what's known as the "Anti-dog-eat-dog rule," prohibiting "cutthroat" competition. The rule puts the superb Phoenix-Durango Railroad, Taggart Transcontinental's competitor for the Colorado freight traffic, out of business. With the Phoenix-Durango line gone, Dagny must rebuild the Rio Norte Line quickly.

Dagny asks Francisco, who is in New York, what his purpose was in building the worthless Mexican mines. He tells her that it was to damage d'Anconia Copper and Taggart Transcontinental, as well as to cause secondary destructive consequences. Dagny is dumbfounded, unable to reconcile such a destructive purpose from the brilliant, productive industrialist Francisco was just ten years earlier. Not long after this conversation, Francisco appears at a celebration for Hank Rearden's wedding anniversary. Rearden's wife Lillian, his mother, and his brother are nonproductive freeloaders who believe that the strong are morally obliged to support the weak. Rearden no longer loves and cannot respect them, but he pities their weakness and carries them on his back. Francisco meets Rearden for the first time and warns him that the freeloaders have a weapon that they are using against him. Rearden questions why Francisco has come to the party, but Francisco says that he merely wished to become acquainted with Rearden. He won't explain his presence any further.

Although public opinion and an incompetent contractor are working against them, Dagny and Rearden build the Rio Norte Line. Rearden designs an innovative bridge for the line that takes advantage of the properties that his new metal possesses. The State Science Institute, a government research organization, tries to bribe and threaten Rearden to keep his metal off the market, but he won't give in. The Institute then issues a statement devoid of factual evidence that alleges possible weaknesses in the structure of Rearden Metal. Taggart stock crashes, the contractor quits, and the railroad union forbids its employees to work on the Rio Norte Line. When Dr. Robert Stadler, a brilliant theoretical scientist in whose name the State Science Institute was founded, refuses to publicly defend Rearden Metal even though he knows its value, Dagny makes a decision. She tells her brother that she will take a leave of absence, form her own company, and build the Rio Norte Line on her own. She signs a contract saying that when the line is successfully completed, she'll turn it back over to Taggart Transcontinental. Dagny chooses to name it the John Galt Line in defiance of the general pessimism that surrounds her.

Rearden and the leading businessmen of Colorado invest in the John Galt Line. Rearden feels a strong sexual attraction to Dagny but, because he regards sex as a demeaning impulse, doesn't act on his attraction. The government passes the Equalization of Opportunity Bill that prevents an individual from owning companies in different fields. The bill prohibits Rearden from owning the mines that supply him with the raw materials he needs to make Rearden Metal. However, Rearden creates a new design for the John Galt Line's Rearden Metal Bridge, realizing that if he combines a truss with an arch, it will enable him to maximize the best qualities of the new metal.

Dagny completes construction of the Line ahead of schedule. She and Rearden ride in the engine cab on the Line's first train run, which is a resounding success. Rearden and Dagny have dinner at Ellis Wyatt's home to celebrate. After dinner, Dagny and Rearden make love for the first time. The next day, Rearden is contemptuous of them both for what he considers their low urges, but Dagny is radiantly happy. She rejects Rearden's estimate, knowing that their sexual attraction is based on mutual admiration for each other's noblest qualities.

Dagny and Rearden go on vacation together, driving around the country looking at abandoned factories. At the ruins of the Twentieth Century Motor Company's factory in Wisconsin, they find the remnant of a motor with the potential to change the world. The motor was able to draw static electricity from the atmosphere and convert it to usable energy, but now it is destroyed.

Realizing how much the motor would benefit the transportation industry, Dagny vows to find the inventor. At the same time, she must fight against new proposed legislation. Various economic pressure groups, seeking to cash in on the industrial success of Colorado, want the government to force the successful companies to share their profits. Dagny knows that the legislation would put Wyatt Oil and the other Colorado companies out of business, destroy the Rio Norte Line, and remove the profit she needs to rebuild the rest of the transcontinental rail system, but she's powerless to prevent the legislation.

Dagny continues her nationwide quest to find the inventor of the motor, and she finally finds the widow of the engineer who ran the automobile company's research department. The widow tells Dagny that a young scientist working for her husband invented the motor. She doesn't know his name, but she provides a clue that leads Dagny to a cook in an isolated Wyoming diner. The cook tells Dagny to forget the inventor of the motor because he won't be found until he chooses. Dagny is shocked to discover that the cook is Hugh Akston, the world's greatest living philosopher. She goes to Cheyenne and discovers that Wesley Mouch, the new economic coordinator of the country, has issued a series of directives that will result in the strangling of Colorado's industrial success. Dagny rushes to Colorado but arrives too late. Ellis Wyatt, in defiance of the government's edict, set fire to his oil wells and retired.

Months later, the situation in Colorado continues to deteriorate. With the Wyatt oil wells out of business, the economy struggles. Several of the other major industrialists have retired and disappeared; nobody knows where they've gone. Dagny is forced to cut trains on the Colorado schedule. The one bright spot of her work is her continued search for the inventor of the motor. She speaks to Robert Stadler who recommends a young scientist, Quentin Daniels of the Utah Institute of Technology, as a man capable of undertaking the motor's reconstruction.

The State Science Institute orders 10,000 tons of Rearden Metal for a top-secret project, but Rearden refuses to sell it to them. Rearden sells to Ken Danagger, the country's best producer of coal, an amount of Rearden Metal that the law deems illegal. Meanwhile, at the reception for James Taggart's wedding, Francisco d'Anconia publicly defends the morality of producing wealth. Rearden overhears what Francisco says and finds himself increasingly drawn to this supposedly worthless playboy. The day following the reception, Rearden's wife discovers that he's having an affair, but she doesn't know with whom. A manipulator who seeks control over her husband, Lillian uses guilt as a weapon against him.

Dr. Ferris of the State Science Institute tells Rearden that he knows of the illegal sale to Ken Danagger and will take Rearden to trial if he refuses to sell the Institute the metal it needs. Rearden refuses, and the government brings charges against himself and Danagger. Dagny, in the meantime, has become convinced that a destroyer is loose in the world—some evil creature that is deliberately luring away the brains of the world for a purpose she cannot understand. Her diligent assistant, Eddie Willers, knows that Dagny's fears are justified. He eats his meals in the workers' cafeteria, where he has befriended a nameless worker. Eddie tells the worker about Dagny's fear that Danagger is next in line for the destroyer—that he'll be the next to retire and disappear. Dagny races to Pittsburgh to meet with Danagger to convince him to stay, but she's too late. Someone has already met with Danagger and convinced him to retire. In a mood of joyous serenity, Danagger tells Dagny that nothing could convince him to remain. The next day, he disappears.

Francisco visits Rearden and empathizes with the pain he has endured because of the invention of Rearden Metal. Francisco begins to ask Rearden what could make such suffering worthwhile when an accident strikes one of Rearden's furnaces. Francisco and Rearden race to the scene and work arduously to make the necessary repairs. Afterward, when Rearden asks him to finish his question, Francisco says that he knows the answer and departs.

At his trial, Rearden states that he doesn't recognize his deal with Danagger as a criminal action and, consequently, doesn't recognize the court's right to try him. He says that a man has the right to own the product of his effort and to trade it voluntarily with others. The government has no moral basis for outlawing the voluntary exchange of goods and services. The government, he says, has the power to seize his metal by force, and they have the power to compel him at the point of a gun. But he won't cooperate with their demands, and he won't pretend that the process is civil. If the government wishes to deal with men by compulsion, it must do so openly. Rearden states that he won't help the government pretend that his trial is anything but the initiation of a forced seizure of his metal. He says that he's proud of his metal, he's proud of his mills, he's proud of every penny that he's earned by his own hard work, and he'll not cooperate by voluntarily yielding one cent that is his. Rearden says that the government will have to seize his money and products by force, just like the robber it is. At this point, the crowd bursts into applause. The judges recognize the truth of what Rearden says and refuse to stand before the American people as open thieves. In the end, they fine Rearden and suspend the sentence.

Because of the new economic restrictions, the major Colorado industrialists have all retired and disappeared. Freight traffic has dwindled, and Taggart Transcontinental has been forced to shut down the Rio Norte Line. The railroad is in terrible condition: It is losing money, the government has convinced James Taggart to grant wage raises, and there is ominous talk that the railroad will be forced to cut shipping rates. At the same time, Wesley Mouch is desperate for Rearden to cooperate with the increasingly dictatorial government. Because Rearden came to Taggart's wedding celebration, Mouch believes that Taggart can influence Rearden. Mouch implies that a trade is possible: If Taggart can convince Rearden to cooperate, Mouch will prevent the government from forcing a cut in shipping rates. Taggart appeals to Lillian for help, and Lillian discovers that Dagny Taggart is her husband's lover.

In response to devastating economic conditions, the government passes the radical Directive 10-289, which requires that all workers stay at their current jobs, all businesses remain open, and all patents and inventions be voluntarily turned over to the government. When she hears the news, Dagny resigns from the railroad. Rearden doesn't resign from Rearden Steel, however, because he has two weeks to sign the certificate turning his metal over to the government, and he wants to be there to refuse when the time is up. Dr. Floyd Ferris of the State Science Institute comes to Rearden and says that the government has evidence of his affair with Dagny Taggart and will make it public—dragging Dagny's name through the gutter—if he refuses to sign over his metal. Rearden now knows that his desire for Dagny is the highest virtue he possesses and is free of all guilt regarding it, but he's a man who pays his own way. He knows that he should have divorced Lillian long ago and openly declared his love for Dagny. His guilt and error gave his enemies this weapon. He must pay for his own error and not allow Dagny to suffer, so he signs.

Dagny has retreated to a hunting lodge in the mountains that she inherited from her father. She's trying to decide what to do with the rest of her life when word reaches her that a train wreck of enormous proportions has destroyed the famed Taggart Tunnel through the heart of the Rockies, making all transcontinental traffic impossible on the main track. She rushes back to New York to resume her duties, and she reroutes all transcontinental traffic. She receives a letter from Quentin Daniels telling her that, because of Directive 10-289, he's quitting. Dagny plans to go west to inspect the track and to talk to Daniels.

On the train ride west, Dagny rescues a hobo who is riding the rails. He used to work for the Twentieth Century Motor Company. He tells her that the company put into practice the communist slogan, "From each according to his ability, to each according to his need," a scheme that resulted in enslaving the able to the unable. The first man to quit was a young engineer, who walked out of a mass meeting saying that he would put an end to this once and for all by "stopping the motor of the world." The bum tells her that as the years passed and they saw factories close, production drop, and great minds retire and disappear, they began to wonder if the young engineer, whose name was John Galt, succeeded.

On her trip west, Dagny's train is stalled when the crew abandons it. She finds an airplane and continues on to Utah to find Daniels, but she learns at the airport that Daniels left with a visitor in a beautiful plane. Realizing that the visitor is the "destroyer," she gives chase, flying among the most inaccessible peaks of the Rockies. Her plane crashes.

Dagny finds herself in Atlantis, the hidden valley to which the great minds have gone to escape the persecution of a dictatorial government. She finds that John Galt does exist and that he's the man she's been seeking in two ways: He is both the inventor of the motor and the "destroyer," the man draining the brains of the world. All the great men she admires are here—inventors, industrialists, philosophers, scientists, and artists. Dagny learns that the brains are on strike. They refuse to think, create, and work in a world that forces them to sacrifice themselves to society. They're on strike against the creed of self-sacrifice, in favor of a man's right to his own life.

Dagny falls in love with Galt, who has loved and watched her for years. But Dagny is a scab, the most dangerous enemy of the strike, and Galt won't touch her—yet. Dagny has the choice to join the strike and remain in the valley or go back to her railroad and the collapsing outside world. She is torn, but she refuses to give up the railroad and returns. Although Galt's friends don't want him to expose himself to the danger, he returns as well, so he can be near at hand when Dagny decides she's had enough.

When she returns, Dagny finds that the government has nationalized the railroad industry and controls it under a Railroad Unification Plan. Dagny can no longer make business decisions based on matters of production and profit; she is subject to the arbitrary whims of the dictators. The government wants Dagny to make a reassuring speech to the public on the radio and threatens her with the revelation of her affair with Rearden. On the air, Dagny proudly states that she was Rearden's lover and that he signed his metal over to the government only because of a blackmail threat. Before being cut off the air, Dagny succeeds in warning the American people about the ruthless dictatorship that the United States government is becoming.

Because of the government's socialist policies, the collapse of the U. S. economy is imminent. Francisco d'Anconia destroys his holdings and disappears because his properties worldwide are about to be nationalized. He leaves the "looters"—the parasites who feed off the producers—nothing, wiping out millions of dollars belonging to corrupt American investors like James Taggart. Meanwhile, politicians use their economic power to create their own personal empires. In one such scheme, the Taggart freight cars needed to haul the Minnesota wheat harvest to market are diverted to a project run by the relatives of powerful politicians. The wheat rots at the Taggart stations, the farmers riot, farms shut down (as do many of the companies providing them with equipment), people lose their jobs, and severe food shortages result.

During an emergency breakdown at the Taggart Terminal in New York City, Dagny finds that John Galt is one of the railroad's unskilled laborers. She sees him in the crowd of men ready to carry out her commands. After completing her task, Dagny walks into the abandoned tunnels, knowing that Galt will follow. They make love for the first time, and he then returns to his mindless labor.

The government smuggles its men into Rearden's mills, pretending that they're steelworkers. The union of steelworkers asks for a raise, but the government refuses, making it sound as if the refusal comes from Rearden. When Rearden rejects the Steel Unification Plan the government wants to spring on him, they use the thugs they've slipped into his mills to start a riot. The pretense of protecting Rearden is the government's excuse for taking over his mills. But Francisco d'Anconia, under an assumed name, has taken a job at Rearden's mills. He organizes the workers, and they successfully defend the mills against the government's thugs. Afterward, Francisco tells Rearden the rest of the things he wants him to know. Rearden retires, disappears, and joins the strike.

Mr. Thompson, the head of state, is set to address the nation regarding its dire economic conditions. But before he begins to speak, he is preempted, cut off the air by a motor of incalculable power. John Galt addresses the nation instead. Galt informs citizens that the men of the mind are on strike, that they require freedom of thought and action, and that they refuse to work under the dictatorship in power. The thinkers won't return, Galt says, until human society recognizes an individual's right to live his own life. Only when the moral code of self-sacrifice is rejected will the thinkers be free to create, and only then will they return.

The government rulers are desperate. Frantically, they seek John Galt. They want him to become economic dictator of the country so the men of the mind will come back and save the government, but Galt refuses. Realizing that Dagny thinks the same way that Galt does, the government has her followed. Mr. Thompson makes clear to Dagny that certain members of the government fear and hate Galt, and that if they find him first, they may kill him. Terrified, Dagny goes to Galt's apartment to see if he's still alive. The government's men follow her and take Galt into custody, and the rulers attempt to convince Galt to take charge of the country's economy. He refuses. They torture him, yet still he refuses. In the end, the strikers come to his rescue. Francisco and Rearden, joined now by Dagny, assault the grounds of the State Science Institute where Galt is held captive. They kill some guards and incapacitate others, release Galt, and return to the valley. Dagny and Galt are united. Shortly after, the final collapse of the looters' regime occurs, and the men of the mind are free to return to the world.

List of Characters

John Galt The main character of the novel, John Galt is the man who dominates the action, though he doesn't appear until two-thirds of the way through the novel. John Galt is the character who conceives, initiates, and carries to a successful conclusion the strike of the great minds that forms the core of the novel's action. He is both the inventor of the motor and the "destroyer" that Dagny fears.

Dagny Taggart The novel's heroine, Dagny Taggart is Galt's most dangerous enemy but also the woman he loves. Dagny is a brilliant engineer/businesswoman who runs a transcontinental railroad expertly. Her strength of purpose and impassioned commitment to the railroad enables her to withstand the injustices of the looters' regime and, by her prodigious productivity, inadvertently sustain that regime. She is the primary foe that Galt must defeat.

Hank Rearden Hank Rearden is the industrialist who runs the country's finest steel mills. Through ten years of herculean effort, he has invented a new substance—Rearden Metal—that is vastly superior to steel. Hank is also Dagny's colleague and lover through much of the story. He is the other great industrialist inadvertently propping up the looters' regime and, consequently, also a danger to Galt's strike. Rearden has uncritically accepted part of the looters' code—the moral premise that an individual has the unchosen obligation to serve others. In order to experience the joy that he has earned, Rearden must liberate himself from the shackles of the self-sacrifice morality.

Francisco d'Anconia A friend and ally of John Galt, Francisco d'Anconia was the first to join Galt in going on strike and is an active recruiting officer for the strike. Francisco is the world's wealthiest man, a brilliant copper industrialist who takes the disguise of a hedonistic playboy as a means of hiding his true intent: the gradual destruction of d'Anconia Copper and of the millions of dollars invested in it by American businessmen. A childhood friend of Dagny's and her first lover, he pays the highest price for his role in the strike.

Ragnar Danneskjöld Like Francisco, Ragnar Danneskjöld is a friend of Galt's who joins the strike at its inception. A brilliant philosopher who chooses to fight the looters as a pirate, he robs their ships and restores the wealth to the people who produced it. Danneskjöld is the opposite of Robin Hood: He robs the poor and gives to the rich—he takes from the parasitical and restores wealth to the productive.

Hugh Akston Hugh Akston is the greatest living philosopher and the last great advocate of reason—or "the first of their return." He taught Galt, Francisco, and Ragnar at the Patrick Henry University, where he was head of the Department of Philosophy. He joins Galt's strike in its early days, leading to the paradox of a great thinker earning his living as a short-order cook at an isolated diner.

Richard Halley Halley is the composer whose works Dagny loves. His music, boasting beautiful melodies and heroic themes, is rejected by a culture that worships depravity. He joins the strike when he comprehends the vast differences between the premises underlying his music and the ideas held by the men in power.

Midas Mulligan The most successful banker in the world, Mulligan owns the valley in a remote section of the Colorado Rockies to which the strikers retire. In the outside world, Mulligan was regarded as greedy and cold-hearted because he based his investments on productive ability, not on need. He joins the strike because he realizes that he loves being alive and that this love cannot be fulfilled in a society that enslaves his mind.

Ellis Wyatt Ellis Wyatt is an innovative entrepreneur of the oil industry. His discovery of a new method for extracting oil from shale rock initiates the economic boom in Colorado. The industries that grow up around Wyatt Oil are the last hope for the country's prosperity. Wyatt is a defiant individualist who refuses to tolerate the destructive policies of the government. Rather than allow the rulers to slowly suck the blood from his business, he sets fires to his wells, resulting in the unquenchable "Wyatt's Torch."

The Colorado Industrialists These men, along with Wyatt, are responsible for the great prosperity achieved in Colorado. Andrew Stockton runs the country's finest foundry. Lawrence Hammond is the last manufacturer on earth of superb automobiles, and Dwight Sanders is a genius of the aviation industry. Likewise, Ted Nielsen of Nielsen Motors and Roger Marsh of Marsh Electric are superb producers of motors and electrical appliances. However, all of them are destroyed by regulations the government imposes on Colorado. All of the Colorado Industrialists recognize the futility of attempting to produce under the socialist policies of the rulers and join Galt's strike seeking freedom.

Ken Danagger Dannager is a Pennsylvania coal producer and friend of Hank Rearden's. Like Rearden, Dannager recognizes the destructive nature of the rulers' laws and breaks them, engaging in illegal deals that are necessary if he wants to keep producing coal. He joins the strike after being arrested for his part in the transaction that results in Rearden's trial.

Judge Narragansett Judge Narragansett is the legal figure who stands for the rule of objective law and the rights of the individual. He joins the strike when he understands that the administration of justice is impossible under the looters' arbitrary decrees. In the end, as the strikers prepare to return, he revises a clause in the United States Constitution, prohibiting the government from enacting laws that abridge the freedom of production and trade.

Dan Conway Dan Conway builds the tiny Phoenix-Durango Railroad into the dominant railroad of the southwestern states. As Taggart Transcontinental deteriorates, Dan Conway's road takes most of the Colorado freight traffic. Because he provides such superb service to his shippers, James Taggart uses political influence to pass the "Anti-dog-eat-dog Rule," putting Conway out of business.

Eddie Willers Dagny's childhood friend and assistant at Taggart Transcontinental, Eddie Willers is a conscientious worker and loyal employee of the railroad who is outraged by the restrictions that the looters place on America's most productive individuals. Through Eddie, the mysterious railroad worker in the cafeteria gains important information regarding Dagny's work, the state of the railroad, and the conditions of American industry.

Cherryl Brooks The poor shop girl who mistakenly idolizes James Taggart and marries him, Cherryl Brooks is a hero worshipper. She admires achievement and the individuals who attain it. Cherryl leaves the slum neighborhood in which she was raised to come to New York City to advance her career. Because of her ambition and her hero worship (her virtues), James Taggart seeks to destroy her. He is powerless to destroy Dagny, Francisco, Rearden, and the others, so he wreaks his hatred of the good on Cherryl.

The Wet Nurse The Wet Nurse is the young bureaucrat just out of college whom the government assigns as a spy to Rearden's mills. Despite being taught nothing but moral relativism by his teachers, the boy is sufficiently honest to recognize Rearden's moral stature and the looters' evil. He grows into a legitimate hero worshipper like Cherryl and, similarly, is destroyed by the looters.

Tom Colby The head of the union of Rearden steelworkers, Tom Colby recognizes that there is no necessary conflict of interest between employer and employees. Rearden demands and gets the most efficient labor force in the world, for which he pays wages significantly above union scale. Colby, a diligent worker, recognizes that Rearden is his ally, not a "class enemy."

Gwen Ives Gwen Ives is Rearden's secretary. She's ruthlessly efficient in her work and intensely loyal to Rearden and his mills. Her commitment to justice is shown when she cries at the news that Rearden has been robbed of his ore mines by the passage of the Equalization of Opportunity Bill. When Rearden retires and disappears, she too leaves the firm.

James Taggart Dagny's older brother and the President of Taggart Transcontinental, Jim is a "looter"—a businessman who seeks gain not by productive work but by political connections. The difference between Dagny and her brother is shown in their reactions to Dan Conway's Phoenix-Durango Railroad. They both want to put the competitor out of business. Dagny wishes to do so by building Taggart's Rio Norte Line into a more efficient road, whereas Jim seeks to destroy the Phoenix-Durango by political decree. Where Dagny stands for production, Jim stands for force. Jim is motivated by his hatred of good men and his desire to kill such individuals as Dagny, Rearden, Francisco, and Galt.

Lillian Rearden Lillian is Hank Rearden's wife. She cultivates connections with the looters in an attempt to reach the one goal of her life—the destruction of the husband she hates. Envy and hatred of the good dominate her, just as they do James Taggart. Her chosen mission in life is destruction, but she's more honest with herself than Taggart is. Taggart attempts to delude himself into believing that he's motivated by a desire for material gain, whereas Lillian Rearden acknowledges that she's motivated solely by a desire to destroy the good that she can never hope to match.

Dr. Robert Stadler The brilliant scientist turned looter-politician, Robert Stadler was once head of the Department of Physics at the Patrick Henry University. A genius in the field of theoretical physics, he was also the teacher of Galt, Francisco, and Ragnar. Stadler believes that most men are irrational and impervious to reason. Because men would never voluntarily choose science, they must be forced to support it. Stadler believes that the men of the mind are an endangered minority among the uneducated masses and should have the right to rule. For this reason, he thinks he can use governmental force to advance the cause of science.

Wesley Mouch The economic dictator of the country, Mouch is an unscrupulous mediocrity who begins his political career as Rearden's "Washington man." He rises by selling Rearden out regarding the Equalization of Opportunity Bill, thereby winning the favor of James Taggart. Taggart's patronage enables Mouch to rise to the top of the economic bureaucracy. In the end, with the country in economic collapse, Mr. Thompson wishes to force Mouch's job on John Galt.

Mr. Thompson Mr. Thompson is the Head of State. He is utterly pragmatic, contemptuous of principles or convictions, and driven by the expediency of the moment. He will make any deal necessary with anybody in order to keep himself in power. Mr. Thompson even believes that he can cut a deal with John Galt who, in his view, has control of a political pressure group—the men of brains. Mr. Thompson is honestly puzzled by Galt's unwillingness to make a deal with him. In his cynical view, there is no such thing as a man not open to a corrupt deal.

Dr. Floyd Ferris The day-to-day head of the State Science Institute, Dr. Floyd Ferris is a murderous bureaucrat with an unquenchable lust for political power. Dr. Ferris would murder Galt without a second thought rather than give up the power he has gained. Ferris postures as a scientist but is actually hostile to the mind, because the thinkers, he recognizes, don't unquestioningly obey a dictator's commands. Therefore, he consistently attacks the mind, as in his book, *Why Do You Think You Think?*

Dr. Simon Pritchett Dr. Simon Pritchett is the professor who takes Hugh Akston's place as head of the Department of Philosophy at Patrick Henry University. Like Ferris, Pritchett is a skeptic, attacking the mind's ability to gain knowledge. When contrasted with Hugh Akston, Dr. Pritchett is an example of the decline of philosophy in an era when the mind is on strike.

Orren Boyle The owner of Associated Steel (a competitor of Rearden's), Boyle is a friend of Jim Taggart's and an unprincipled businessman who seeks gain solely by virtue of his connections in Washington. The government's expropriation of patents gives Boyle the legal right to manufacture Rearden Metal, but Ragnar Danneskjöld blows up his mills, ensuring that the only man to profit from the new metal is the one who created it.

Fred Kinnan The head of the country's labor unions, Kinnan is a gangster who seeks only power and plunder from his position. However, he's the most honest of the looters. Most of the looters try to convince themselves that they enslave the country for the "public good." Kinnan openly admits that he's just a criminal seeking the unearned.

Character Web

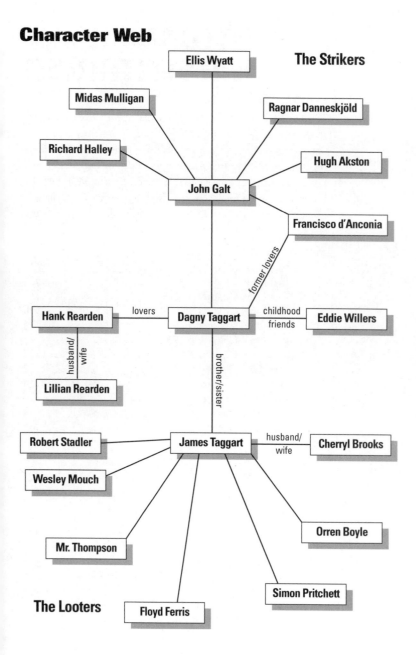

CRITICAL COMMENTARIES

The following Introduction section is provided solely as an educational tool and is not meant to replace the experience of your reading the work. Read the Introduction and A Brief Synopsis to enhance your understanding of the work and to prepare yourself for the critical thinking that should take place whenever you read any work of fiction or nonfiction. Keep the List of Characters and Character Map at hand so that as you read the original literary work, if you encounter a character about whom you're uncertain, you can refer to the List of Characters and Character Map to refresh your memory.

Part One
Chapter 1—The Theme

Summary

Eddie Willers, special assistant to the vice president in charge of operations of Taggart Transcontinental Railroad, is accosted by a bum on the streets of New York City, who asks him, "Who is John Galt?" The question is an expression of futility—a slang phrase that indicates a hopeless situation. Eddie doesn't like the question, just as he doesn't like to see shops closing along Fifth Avenue and other previously prosperous streets. He is troubled by the steadily declining revenues of the railroad and the diminishing industrial output of the country in general.

Eddie speaks to James Taggart, president of the railroad, regarding the desperate condition of the track on their Rio Norte Line that serves Colorado, the last state whose industrial production is booming. He reminds Jim that Colorado—the home of Ellis Wyatt, whose discovery of a new method of extracting oil from shale rock led to the boom—is vital to the country's survival and can't be left without transportation. Taggart Transcontinental needs new rail now. Jim says that his friend Orren Boyle, the head of Associated Steel, has experienced unavoidable delays in the production of his rail and can't be blamed. Eddie says that Hank Rearden of Rearden Steel, the last great steel producer in the country, can provide the rails. Taggart refuses to consider Eddie's proposition.

Jim's sister and Eddie's boss, Dagny Taggart, returns from a trip to examine the Rio Norte Line. Dagny found the line in worse shape than she expected. She tells Jim that she has cancelled the order with Associated Steel and placed it with Rearden. Dagny has ordered rail made not of steel but of a new product, Rearden Metal. Jim objects on the grounds that the new metal has never been tried before and hasn't been approved by public opinion. Dagny, who studied engineering in college, tells him that she has seen Rearden's formula and tests, and she's convinced that Rearden's invention is superior to steel. Dagny also says that she'll use Rearden Metal to rebuild the Rio Norte Line and win back shippers from Dan Conway's superb Phoenix-Durango Railroad, which now carries most of Colorado's freight traffic. She's determined to save the railroad from the consequences of Jim's policies, especially his construction of the worthless San Sebastian Line which, she asserts, the socialist Mexican government will imminently nationalize.

Other things besides her brother's destructive policies disturb Dagny. For example, she wants to promote Owen Kellogg, an efficient employee of the Terminal Division, but he quits and leaves the railroad industry entirely. Furthermore, Dagny heard a young brakeman on her returning train whistling a theme that sounded like a composition of Richard Halley, the composer whose works she loves. But Halley retired suddenly eight years ago and disappeared. When she questioned the brakeman regarding the new piece, he replied that it was Halley's Fifth Concerto. After she reminded him that Halley wrote only four, he became evasive. Dagny calls the company that publishes Halley's music and finds that he hasn't written a new piano concerto.

Commentary

The American economy is gradually collapsing. Industrial production is in steady decline, stores are closing, and workers are unemployed. A general gloominess pervades the culture, giving rise to the rhetorical question, "Who is John Galt?" The question expresses the widespread belief that no one can answer the difficult questions facing the American society. Dagny and Eddie contemptuously reject this pessimistic attitude and fight it.

Ayn Rand sets up a contrast immediately between Dagny, the story's heroine, and her brother, Jim. Both are businesspeople, but each holds markedly different moral and political theories. Dagny is a model of the spirit and practice of capitalism. She believes in industrial production and profit—hard work and earning large amounts of money. She orders rails from Hank Rearden instead of Orren Boyle because Rearden delivers his product and Boyle does not. Likewise, Dagny will provide freight service to Ellis Wyatt and the Colorado industrialists but not to the destitute economy of socialist Mexico because Wyatt and his colleagues produce but the Mexican economy does not. Jim, on the other hand, is an example of the spirit and practice of socialism. He believes in sacrificing for the "public good" and in giving chances to the little guy, rather than dealing with those already successful. He orders rail from Associated Steel instead of the efficient Rearden Steel in order, he says, to give Orren Boyle a chance.

Likewise, Jim builds the San Sebastian Line at a cost of millions to give the impoverished Mexicans an economic opportunity. Dagny seeks to earn profit; Jim seeks to serve the public welfare. Because of their underlying differences, Dagny and Jim clash regarding the San Sebastian Line, the choice of steel companies, and many other things.

Jim lacks a mind of his own. Public opinion is an important consideration for him. For example, he's afraid to take a chance on Rearden Metal because the product is new and not yet accepted by society. Jim Taggart isn't a man willing to trust his own judgment, and he's not one to innovate or take a chance on inventions or new methods. Dagny, on the other hand, isn't concerned with what people believe or say. She has a mind of her own and follows her own judgment. For example, she studies Rearden's formula and examines the results of his testing in order to understand the metal's superiority. Dagny is a rigorous engineer concerned only with the facts of the metal and its capabilities, not with the public's beliefs or fears. Dagny says that she'll take full responsibility for the metal's performance, and Jim finally agrees to the purchase of Rearden metal rails. Dagny stakes her future on her own judgment.

This chapter also shows the ominous collapse of American industrial production. The closing plants and stores, the rising unemployment, and the lack of consumer goods aren't the only elements adding to the growing gloom. The retirement and mysterious disappearance of brilliant, talented individuals in a wide range of fields adds to society's pessimistic outlook. For example, Richard Halley, the brilliant composer whose music Dagny loves, has retired and gone into seclusion. Likewise, Owen Kellogg, a rising young star of Taggart Transcontinental, tells Dagny that he's leaving not only the Taggart line, but railroading entirely. He loves his work, and he doesn't plan a career in another field, but he leaves. Owen's reasons are a mystery to Dagny; she finds his actions inexplicable.

The question of the new piece of music also troubles her. She knows with certainty that only Richard Halley could've written the melody that the young Taggart brakeman whistled. But the boy's attitude became evasive when Dagny reminded him that Halley wrote only four piano concertos. And the publisher of his music assures her that Halley is retired and has stopped writing. There is no fifth Halley concerto. What, then, was the young brakeman whistling? Why did he tell her it was Halley's Fifth and then retract his claim?

The steady decline of American prosperity reminds Eddie Willers of the oak tree that stood on the Taggart estate when he was a child. The tree was huge and powerful and stood for centuries. In fact, Eddie thought that it would always stand there. Its roots were deeply embedded in the soil, and Eddie thought that if a giant grabbed the tree, he would be unable to uproot it but would swing the hill and the entire earth with it "like a ball at the end of a string." The youthful Eddie thought of the oak tree as a symbol of strength and solidity and felt safe in its presence. However, lightning struck the tree. When Eddie looked into its trunk, he discovered that the interior had rotted away long ago. The trunk was merely an empty shell, no longer containing living power. The adult Eddie experiences the same feeling when walking into the Taggart Building. He always felt safe there, in the midst of its great power and its capacity to provide train service to a continent. But now when he walks into the president's office—the heart of the building and of the railroad—Eddie doesn't find the energy of a great living power. Instead, he finds the deadly inner corruption that is James Taggart.

Literary Device

The oak tree, giving the appearance of strength and vitality, is a symbol to Eddie. It reminds him that things aren't always what they seem—particularly that the outward appearance of power isn't necessarily an accurate indication of inner reality. Taggart Transcontinental (and the U.S. economy in a more general sense), although powerful and seemingly safe through many years, has now rotted away. Eddie wonders what is causing the deterioration.

Glossary

Who is John Galt? This phrase is uttered as a sign of despair and hopelessness. The question lacks specific meaning and cannot be answered. Its use in everyday language is a sign that people believe answers don't exist to the problems that plague American society. Dagny and (to a lesser extent) Eddie are dynamic thinkers and people of action who believe that answers are possible and that positive steps can be taken to save American society. Consequently, they reject the pessimism that this question embodies.

Rearden Metal This is the new substance created by steel industrialist Hank Rearden after ten years of demanding effort. The new
metal is lighter, stronger, and cheaper than steel. Although its innovative nature frightens people and it hasn't been accepted yet, Rearden and Dagny both know that this product will revolutionize
industrial production.

Part One
Chapter 2—The Chain

Summary

Hank Rearden pours the first heat for his first order of Rearden Metal. As he walks home from his office late that night, Rearden thinks about the ten years of excruciating effort that went into inventing his new metal. We learn that he has been working since he was 14 years old, starting in the ore mines of Minnesota. With exhausting labor over a period of decades, he rose to own the ore mines. Now he owns steel mills as well.

The first thing that Rearden made from the first heat of Rearden Metal was a bracelet for his wife, Lillian. When he arrives home, he gives Lillian the bracelet. Lillian, his mother, and his unemployed brother—who all reside with Rearden and live off his income—insult him. The trio tries to make Rearden feel guilty for the hours that he works and his love of the company, and they accuse him of neglecting them. Lillian looks at the bracelet, which is shaped like a chain, and remarks, "A chain. Appropriate, isn't it? It's the chain by which he holds us all in bondage."

Paul Larkin, an unsuccessful businessman who claims to look up to Rearden, warns him regarding the state of his public relations. Larkin says that the newspapers depict Rearden as an antisocial enemy of the people, interested only in running steel mills and earning a profit. Rearden says that the newspapers are right about his love for his business. Larkin hints at possible political dangers and warns Rearden to make sure that his "Washington man," the political lobbyist he pays to protect him from the legislation of the socialist rulers, is loyal.

Commentary

This chapter establishes several important points regarding Rearden and his family. Rearden is an innovative metallurgist who, by means of herculean labor over a ten-year period, created a new metal that will revolutionize industrial production. Like all great creative minds,

Rearden is motivated by his love of the work (constructive action in the field of his choice). His work—both as a manufacturer of steel and as the inventor of Rearden Metal—is enormously beneficial to his fellow man every day. This fact pleases Rearden, but it's not his driving motive. His motivation is the creative effort itself, his love of doing the work. The positive results that his fellow man accrues are a felicitous secondary consequence.

Character Insight

With the character of Hank Rearden, Ayn Rand makes a point regarding the nature of creative individuals. Rearden is similar to the great inventors, industrialists, writers, and artists of history. The Edisons and Wright Brothers, the Carnegies and Rockefellers, the Shakespeares and Michelangelos all created works that significantly benefitted mankind. Whether through the electric light or the airplane, the production of steel or oil, or the creation of brilliant poetry or sculpture, these great minds have been the benefactors of human society. But, like Rearden, these creative geniuses are driven primarily by their love of their work—by their passionate fascination with a specific field of endeavor. Rearden, and all original thinkers like him, are self-driven, self-motivated, and self-actualized. They aren't slaves to others, nor do they think of themselves as such. Rearden is *selfish*, not in the conventional sense of his family's accusations (meaning uncaring toward others) but in Ayn Rand's sense of being motivated by his own values and happiness.

Character Insight

However, Rearden isn't fully consistent in his commitment to himself. In his work, he has created an unremitting source of joy, but in his marriage and family life, he acts selflessly. His wife and family members are unemployed parasites who live on his generosity and criticize him relentlessly for his indifference toward them. Their accusations have only one purpose: to make Rearden feel guilty. They want him to feel guilty for his ability, initiative, success, money, pride, and happiness. Rearden's family wants him to feel responsible for their feelings of helplessness, misery, and despair. If they can convince him, at some unspoken level, that he is the reason their lives are empty, Rearden will be malleable clay in their hands; they'll be able to control him. Unfortunately, Rearden feels an obligation to them. Although they contribute nothing to his life but more burdens to carry, he believes that he must take care of them. Rearden has accepted the code of *altruism*, the moral theory that claims that the able have the responsibility of caring for the unable. Consequently, he gives to them endlessly without receiving anything positive in return, without asking for or expecting any reciprocation. Because of his self-sacrificial code of ethics regarding his personal relationships, Rearden tolerates the injustice that his family perpetrates on him.

Paul Larkin's warning indicates that the press holds the same moral code as Rearden's family. The press writes that Rearden is selfish and antisocial because he's proud of his mills and runs them himself. The press resents the same things about Rearden—his creative drive, his success, and his pride—that his family does. But Rearden feels strong and laughs off the press attacks. His abundance of productive energy allows him to feel that he can afford to be tolerant of the media.

Larkin urges him to make sure that his protective man in Washington is loyal, but Rearden doesn't take the warning seriously. Because he accepts the premise that a productive man is obligated to carry the needy on his back, Rearden doesn't yet recognize the evil of those who attack him for his success. Consequently, he makes no effort to answer the vicious accusations of his family or the false smears of the press. At this point in the story, Rearden is a great man willing to bear guilt for his virtues and to accept the responsibility of supporting parasites who seek to control him. Rearden needs to be liberated from his acceptance of the self-sacrifice ethics.

Glossary

Rearden's "Washington man" The "Washington man" is a lobbyist Rearden must employ to protect his business from proposed anti-capitalist legislation. In a mixed economy such as contemporary America, there is a combination of freedom and government controls (capitalism and socialism). Rearden owns his mills, but the government has the right to control, regulate, and even expropriate his business. To protect himself, Rearden must hire a man with political connections to plead with the politicians on his behalf. As Rearden points out, the men available for such a job are an unprincipled lot.

The chain The chain is actually the bracelet in the shape of a chain that Rearden gives to Lillian. She claims that it's symbolic of the bondage in which Rearden keeps his family. Lillian has properly identified the nature of the relationship, but this chapter raises the question of who is in bondage to whom.

Part One
Chapter 3—The Top and the Bottom

Summary

Over drinks in a New York bar, four men conduct a meeting that will greatly impact the U.S. economy. Orren Boyle wants Jim Taggart to use his influence with various Washington politicians to pass legislation that will strip Rearden of his ore mines. Taggart agrees to do it. Taggart and Boyle are counting on Paul Larkin, who is present at the meeting, to receive the mines from Rearden and to provide Boyle with first claim on the ore. Taggart, meanwhile, wants Boyle to speak to friends on the National Alliance of Railroads regarding the competition that Dan Conway's Phoenix-Durango Railroad gives Taggart Transcontinental in Colorado. Taggart wants the Alliance to force the Phoenix-Durango out on the grounds that it provides "cutthroat competition" to Taggart Transcontinental in a region where the latter company has historical priority. Boyle states that Taggart's idea is sound, and he'll speak to his friends about it. The fourth member of the party is Wesley Mouch, Rearden's Washington man. In return for not reporting the proposed legislation to Rearden, Mouch will receive a bureaucratic post in Washington, courtesy of Taggart's influence.

Taggart comes to his sister's office. Boyle has told him that on a recent trip to the San Sebastian Mines in Mexico, he observed the limited and archaic train service that Taggart Transcontinental provides. Boyle questions the level of service provided. Dagny reminds Jim of several facts. The San Sebastian Mines, built by Francisco d'Anconia, have produced no copper. Francisco never even presented facts to support the claim that any copper exists there; Jim and his friends invested money based only on Francisco's business reputation. And, in the past ten years, Francisco has degenerated from a remarkable businessman into a worthless playboy. Dagny tells Jim that she's shipped every piece of railroad property that can be moved north of the border, so that when the Mexican government nationalizes the San Sebastian Line, the railroad's loss will be minimal.

Dagny's assistant, Eddie Willers, often eats his meals with a railroad worker in the employees' cafeteria of the Taggart Terminal. He doesn't know the worker's name or job, but because of his rough, grease-stained clothes, Eddie assumes that the job is menial. However, the worker has a deep interest in the railroad, and Eddie feels comfortable speaking to him. He tells the worker that the Rio Norte Line will save Taggart Transcontinental and that Dagny has found a reliable contractor to rebuild the line—McNamara of Cleveland.

Commentary

This chapter shows readers the way things work in a mixed economy that's moving toward socialism. Private property exists nominally, but the state has steadily increasing control over its use and distribution. In such a system, productive businessmen like Hank Rearden and Dan Conway have no rights; they are at the mercy of any inferior competitor with political friends. Only capitalism provides the economic freedom that great producers like Rearden and Conway require. Under a capitalist society, their productive activities would be unrestricted by government bureaucrats and envious competitors.

The men who meet at the beginning of this chapter insist that the preservation of the steel industry "as a whole" is vital to the public welfare. Therefore, Boyle's virtually bankrupt company must not be allowed to fail. It must be propped up by stripping Rearden of his ore mines and turning them over to Paul Larkin, who will please the Washington planners by giving Boyle first priority for the ore. Rearden's productive company will be sacrificed to Boyle's unproductive one, in keeping with the moral premise underlying socialism, which states that the strong must serve the weak.

As the government acquires power over an economy, the level of corruption necessarily rises. This rise in corruption occurs because, as the state gains power to dispense economic favors, it attracts power-seekers like Wesley Mouch and enables incompetent businessmen like Jim Taggart and Orren Boyle to exist parasitically off of competent men like Rearden. In a free market, where customers can choose unrestrictedly among competitors, customers select companies like Rearden's and Dan Conway's because they get the job done. In a free market, businesspeople like Boyle and Taggart go out of business. But in a state-dominated system, unprincipled businesspeople curry favor with power-seeking politicians, brokering corrupt deals that allow them to stay in business by means of legislation.

In contrast to these unprincipled and incompetent businessmen, Dagny fumes over the corruption and mindless incompetence of a statist economic system. As an engineer, she respects the facts. She makes business decisions based on facts, not political favors. She knows that Francisco d'Anconia showed no evidence to support his claim that the San Sebastian Mines contain any copper. Her brother Jim was eager to build a branch line to the mines at a cost of millions to the struggling railroad so that he could please his political "friends" in Washington. The government regards the branch line as a self-sacrificing, "public-spirited" action to aid the destitute Mexicans. As a result of Jim's decision, Taggart Transcontinental will lose millions of dollars—money desperately needed to rebuild the collapsing Rio Norte Line and save the industrial enterprises of Colorado. Dagny tries to reason with her brother and with the men of Taggart Transcontinental's board, but the government's power over the railroad has become too great. She fights a losing battle.

Character Insight

This chapter also hints at Francisco d'Anconia's past, implying that as a young man, he turned his extraordinary talents to industrial production and was fabulously successful. Jim's remarks indicate that Dagny's relationship with Francisco in the past may have been much closer than it is currently. This chapter raises questions about Francisco's true nature, his motives, and his past relationship with Dagny. We don't yet have answers to any of these questions.

Glossary

Progressive policies Progressive policies, in this book, are socialist acts of legislation such as the expropriation of Rearden's ore mines by the government and their distribution to "needy" men like Paul Larkin. The term *progressive,* in matters of economic policy, is a euphemism here for the government's theft of private property and the country's gradual decline into dictatorship. "Progressive" is usually associated with "favoring, working for, or characterized by progress or improvement, as through political or social reform, (or) of or having to do with a person, movement, etc. thought of as being modern or advanced, as in ideas, methods, etc."

Part One
Chapter 4—The Immovable Movers

Summary

McNamara quits. He was the best contractor in the country and the man that Dagny counted on to complete the Rio Norte Line. McNamara walks out on a pile of contracts, and nobody knows why or where he went. The People's State of Mexico nationalizes both the San Sebastian Mines and the San Sebastian Railroad. In his report to the board, James Taggart takes credit for Dagny's decision to move north of the border every piece of railroad equipment that could be transported.

The National Alliance of Railroads passes the Anti-dog-eat-dog Rule, which, as its principal consequence, will cause the Phoenix-Durango Railroad to shut down its Colorado operation within nine months. When Dagny hears of the Rule, she rushes to see Dan Conway, president of the Phoenix-Durango, and urges him to fight the resolution. But Conway responds that he joined the Alliance and voluntarily agreed to follow the majority ruling; he encourages Dagny to repair the Rio Norte Line as quickly as possible, because people like Ellis Wyatt can't be left without transportation. Later, Ellis Wyatt bursts into Dagny's office and informs her that just because Taggart Transcontinental pulled a rotten trick to get rid of its competitor, he won't accept the railroad's current inferior service. Wyatt tells Dagny that if the railroad expects to make money carrying the oil he produces, it must run its business as efficiently as he runs his. Dagny tells Wyatt that he'll have the transportation his company requires.

Dagny tells Rearden that she now needs the rail for the new railroad over a nine-month period, rather than the twelve months of her original plan. Rearden tells her that she'll have the rail. Rearden believes that he and Dagny are a pair of scoundrels who only care about industrial production and profit-making and that they are devoid of any spiritual qualities. But, he concludes, whatever else they may be, they are the people who get things done and move the world.

Commentary

The retirement and disappearance of McNamara adds to the mystery of the story. Why are talented and accomplished individuals leaving? Where are they going? Who is responsible for it? Nobody knows the answers to these questions yet. McNamara was the best contractor in the country, and his sudden retirement makes it significantly more difficult for Dagny to complete the Rio Norte Line.

The Anti-dog-eat-dog Rule is the logical result of a mixed economy—one in the process of rejecting capitalism. When the government has the power to control and regulate private business, it's in a position to dispense economic favors. For example, Jim Taggart can get what he wants from the National Alliance of Railroads in exchange for influencing the politicians to pass legislation that will rob Rearden and benefit Orren Boyle. Boyle makes this point when he sees Taggart after the Alliance votes to approve the Anti-dog-eat-dog Rule. "I've delivered," he says. "Your turn now, Jimmy." Boyle's meaning is clear: He has used his connections in the Alliance to influence the vote, enabling James Taggart to kill the Phoenix-Durango line. Now it's Taggart's turn to return the favor. Taggart must use his political connections to convince the legislature to pass a law that will strip Rearden of his ore mines. The plan is to sign the ore mines over to Paul Larkin, who will give Boyle first claim on the ore.

The corrupt deal brokered by James Taggart and Orren Boyle will harm Hank Rearden and Dan Conway in order to serve the short-term interests of Taggart Transcontinental and Boyle's Associated Steel. Productive men like Rearden and Conway stand to lose either the bulk of or an important component of their businesses, which are torn from them to feed scavengers like James Taggart and Orren Boyle. Men like Rearden and Conway produce value by means of their own effort; they require only freedom to do it. They don't run to the government for favors or handouts, and they don't believe in granting such power to the government. Conversely, parasites like Taggart and Boyle seek to benefit from governmental coercion, because they are too incompetent to compete in a free market. Customers value the products of their superior competitors, and that threatens their livelihood. For example, Colorado shippers prefer Phoenix-Durango to Taggart Transcontinental, and the consumers of steel prefer Rearden's product and service to Boyle's. Rand wants to show that a socialist system always harms the most productive members of society as a means of benefiting the short-term interests of the less productive. The necessary result is a steadily declining standard of living.

Rand also uses the passage of the Anti-dog-eat-dog Rule to illustrate the error of believing in majority rule. A group is merely a collection of individuals, and just as one individual may be mistaken, so may be any number of other individuals. For example, the majority once believed that the sun revolved around the flat earth. The will of a majority is insufficient to make a belief either true or morally right, and such is the case with the proposal ratified by the National Alliance of Railroads. The purpose of the ratified proposal is to rob one of the most productive members of the Alliance (Dan Conway) to benefit the least productive (James Taggart). In this chapter, Rand proves that a man must use his own most scrupulous judgment to arrive at what is true and right, because the blind acceptance of the majority's belief doesn't provide the answer. For example, a rational man like Dan Conway should not agree to abide by the will of a majority or, if he has already done so, he must rescind his agreement when the group demands that he commit suicide. The concept of majority rule is a form of *collectivism,* the belief that an individual must subordinate himself to the group. Rand's claim throughout this book is that an individual must conduct his life in accordance with his own rational thinking; he must not surrender his mind to the majority.

Another important theme continued in this chapter is the inner struggle of Hank Rearden. In the midst of discussing the virtues of Rearden Metal with Dagny, he asserts that the two of them are blackguards because they only care about making money. "We haven't any spiritual goals," he says. "All we're after is material things." Dagny, of course, repudiates this thought. She feels concerned that Rearden should have such an unjust view of himself. Rearden holds a premise that undercuts his potential and prevents him from recognizing the full greatness of his own achievements. He believes that the things of the body—including the creation of new metals—are vulgar and low, lacking all higher "spiritual" qualities. He believes that the more noble purposes of the spirit are devoid of material or bodily concerns. But despite his error—which proceeds from an essentially religious way of thinking—Rearden understands that productive individuals such as himself and Dagny carry the world forward. Men depend on them for material progress.

Glossary

The Immovable Movers The immovable mover is one who causes motion. The term refers to productive giants such as Dagny Taggart and Hank Rearden who, because they generate their own action, carry the world forward. Immovable movers are the rare individuals who hold and pursue a new vision of life's possibilities and are responsible for innovations and progress.

Part One
Chapter 5—The Climax of the d'Anconias

Summary

The government of Mexico is outraged to find that Francisco d'Anconia's San Sebastian Mines are worthless, containing no copper. Francisco is in New York, ostensibly to witness the spectacle of a divorce scandal in which he's supposedly involved. Dagny suspects that Francisco is visiting New York to observe the consequences of the San Sebastian fiasco. On her way to visit him in his hotel room, she thinks about the extraordinary individual he was in his youth. Francisco's genius and exalted view of life's possibilities made him Dagny's dearest companion and her only lover. She can't reconcile her memories with the dissolute playboy he now seems to be.

Francisco tells Dagny that the mine disaster resulted from his lack of effort; he put no thought into the project. Francisco is amused by the fact that his $15 million investment wiped out $40 million belonging to Taggart Transcontinental, $35 million belonging to stockholders like James Taggart and Orren Boyle, and hundreds of millions in such secondary consequences as James Taggart's destruction of the Phoenix-Durango. Dagny can't conceive a reason why any man, much less Francisco d'Anconia, would engage in such deliberate destruction.

Commentary

Literary Device

This chapter adds to the mystery that Rand is building. How can a genius of Francisco's stature sink $15 million of his own money into a worthless project? How can a man who formerly worshipped production now enjoy the destruction of industrial enterprises? Dagny can't fathom the reasons. Many people in this book utter the phrase, "Who is John Galt?," but the question raised in this chapter is, "Who is Francisco d'Anconia?" What could induce such a giant to degenerate into a dissolute playboy and, far worse, an engine of destruction? At this point in the story, an answer to the question doesn't yet exist.

Part One
Chapter 6—The Non-Commercial

Summary

Lillian throws a party for the Reardens' wedding anniversary. Hank Rearden doesn't feel like celebrating but, of course, duty dictates that he must attend. He would prefer to devote his time to the mills, because the superintendent of his rolling mills has resigned suddenly and without explanation. Rearden must find a suitable replacement quickly, because the mills are rolling the Taggart rail.

Dagny attends the party and feels that she and Rearden have legitimate cause to celebrate the Rearden Metal track that's progressing across Colorado. She is puzzled and mildly disappointed when Rearden treats her with rigid formality.

Francisco appears unexpectedly, and Rearden tells his wife that he doesn't wish to meet him. However, Francisco approaches him with such simple sincerity that Rearden speaks to him. Francisco says that Rearden's family wields a weapon against Rearden that he must learn to recognize. Francisco adds that it is crucial for Rearden to take a stand and tell his family that he works for his own happiness. Although Francisco won't explain the purpose behind his appearance at the party or his advice, he claims that he wants to arm Rearden with ideas that he'll need in order to defend himself. Rearden recognizes that Francisco is offering him something crucial, but he also despises this playboy because he squanders his talents and lives an unproductive life. Rearden ends the conversation by insulting Francisco.

At the party, Dagny overhears Lillian's criticism of the Rearden Metal bracelet that Hank gave her. Dagny offers Lillian a diamond bracelet in exchange, which Lillian accepts. The two women exchange angry words and Rearden sides with his wife. Also, several guests at the anniversary celebration discuss the activities of Ragnar Danneskjöld in Delaware Bay. Danneskjöld is a modern pirate who preys on ships carrying welfare payments from the United States to the Peoples' States around the world. No one has been able to catch him.

Commentary

The most important event in this chapter is the meeting of Hank Rearden and Francisco d'Anconia. Francisco is a squandering playboy whom Rearden—a man who has risen from poverty by means of his own backbreaking effort—despises. Rearden wants to completely avoid Francisco, but the dignity of Francisco's manner and the startling truth of his words attract Hank despite his resistance. Francisco's message to Rearden is deceptively simple: It's important for Rearden to announce the egoistic basis of his work and his life to his family and the world. Rearden is egoistic regarding his work because he pursues his values, his loves, and his happiness. He would never sacrifice what is dearest to him (his mills) to his family or to society. However, Rearden isn't egoistic regarding his personal life. He permits a gaggle of vicious moochers to sponge off of him, and he tolerates their moral condemnation. He accepts guilt as payment for his extraordinary achievements. His family abuses him relentlessly for his greatest virtue—his enormous productivity—and he allows their abuse. He gets no happiness or value from his family—only suffering. Because he accepts the morality of self-sacrifice, Rearden willingly carries these parasites on his back. Francisco warns that Rearden must understand and announce to his mooching family that he has no moral obligation to support them—that he does so only out of generosity and kindness, which deserves appreciation and thanks.

Francisco indicates that Rearden is virtuous and a moral paragon *because* of his industriousness, not in spite of it. Rearden must understand his own greatness. He must embrace a joyous pride in his life-giving achievements and reject any guilt that his family asks him to feel. Francisco offers Rearden the beginnings of validation and a moral sanction that Rearden doesn't yet fully realize he needs. Rearden doesn't even have the words yet to define his situation, but somehow he knows that he needs the sanction that Francisco offers.

Dagny's attendance at the party, the beauty of her appearance, and her disappointment at Rearden's indifference reveal her romantic attraction to him. Rearden's rigid formality, and the way he takes Lillian's side regarding the bracelet, offers his own subtle indication that he has similar feelings for Dagny. Rearden holds himself to the strictest standards of justice. Despite the fact that he feels only contempt for Lillian, she is his wife. Rearden realizes that he made a terrible mistake in marrying her, but that mistake is a lifetime commitment that he intends to honor.

The incident with the bracelet emphasizes the contrast between Lillian, whom Rearden barely tolerates, and Dagny, who represents everything Rearden admires. Dagny loves the bracelet made of Rearden Metal because it symbolizes everything she worships—technological innovation, industrial production, and the ability of a man's mind to create progress and prosperity. Lillian, who claims to have higher spiritual concerns, despises the bracelet as something materialistic. Rearden's attraction to Dagny is a threat to his commitment to Lillian; it puts him in danger of committing adultery. At this point in the story, he resists his attraction. Consequently, he treats Dagny coldly in all settings that don't relate directly to business.

The unfolding mystery that lies at the heart of the story continues in this chapter. The superintendent of Rearden's rolling mills resigns without explanation at the precise time that the Rearden Metal rails for the Rio Norte Line are rolled. Francisco offers no explanation for attempting to morally arm Rearden against his family. The world is at the mercy of an invincible pirate who preys on government relief ships, and the combined navies of the world are powerless to catch him. Why has Rearden's superintendent resigned at this crucial time? What is Francisco's purpose in coming to Rearden's moral rescue? Why does the pirate rob the ships of the poor? As of yet, we have no answers to these questions.

Part One
Chapter 7—The Exploiters and the Exploited

Summary

Dagny goes to the construction site of the Rio Norte Line to supervise the work because Ben Nealy, the contractor she found to replace the retired McNamara, is incompetent. Ellis Wyatt arrives, and the respectful manner with which he treats Dagny shows his recognition of the merit of her work. She discovers that Wyatt has been to the job site often and has helped offset Nealy's inefficiency. Rearden is also in Colorado on business of his own. He proposes to Dagny a bridge made of Rearden Metal to replace the old one that the railroad currently maintains. He shows her a design for a new truss that Rearden Metal makes possible, and Dagny agrees to build it.

Dr. Potter of the State Science Institute visits Rearden, informing him that the Institute does not want Rearden Metal to appear on the market at this time. Potter won't state the reasons for this request. When Rearden refuses, Potter offers him unlimited money in exchange for the rights to the metal. Rearden tells him to leave, but Potter gives him a warning: The Institute may issue a public denunciation of the metal. Furthermore, Potter reminds Rearden that the Institute is a government agency and that bills currently pending in the legislature would, if passed, harm Rearden's interests. The legislative votes will be close and may be swayed by Rearden's cooperation.

Rearden throws Dr. Potter out, and the State Science Institute publicly smears Rearden Metal. Its denunciation contains no shred of factual evidence based on laboratory research, focusing instead on innuendoes and unsupported assertions. Dagny visits Dr. Robert Stadler, head of the Institute. Stadler recognizes the contemptible nature of the Institute's statement, but he refuses to publicly state the truth regarding Rearden Metal. His reasons are clear: The public demands practical results in return for its funding, but the Institute's metallurgical department has created nothing of value. If a private individual produces a new metal that is tremendously successful, the public will question the need for a State Science Institute. Stadler will not put the Institute's funding at risk.

The stock of Taggart Transcontinental plummets because of the State Science Institute's attack on Rearden Metal. Dagny tells Jim that she will start her own company to complete the construction of the Rio Norte Line. She says that after the merit of the Rearden Metal track has been proven, the line's ownership will go to Taggart Transcontinental. Jim approves, and Dagny decides to call her railroad the John Galt Line. Rearden and the producers from Colorado invest in her company.

The legislature passes the Equalization of Opportunity Bill, which will strip Rearden of his ore mines and place their ownership in the hands of someone else. Wesley Mouch, Rearden's Washington man, didn't inform Rearden that the bill was being brought to the floor.

Commentary

Theme

This chapter pits those people who are exploited against those who exploit. The State Science Institute, because it cannot match Rearden's achievement, seeks to keep his metal off the market so it doesn't lose credibility with the public. When Rearden refuses to give in to its pleas, bribes, or threats, the Institute denounces his metal, igniting a public response against Rearden. He and Dagny must struggle even harder to complete the John Galt Line on schedule. Furthermore, the government passes the Equalization of Opportunity Bill, prohibiting Rearden from owning any business other than his steel mills and requiring him to relinquish his ore mines. Despite the government's relentless persecution, Rearden creates a new bridge design that will take full advantage of his metal's properties. This chapter sets the creative abilities of two great industrialists in direct conflict with the destructive power of the increasingly socialist government.

Character Insight

Dagny and Rearden represent pure capitalism in action. They are innovative businesspeople, like the productive giants of American history. Rearden's invention of a new metal and Dagny's recognition of its merit reflect the independent thinking so prevalent among the great American industrialists. Henry Ford, for example, perfected the new technique of mass production, bringing the automobile to millions of customers. Thomas Edison invented an electric lighting system that changed the world and earned him millions of dollars. Pioneering industrialists like George Westinghouse, George Eastman, Andrew Carnegie, James J. Hill, and many others performed similar feats. In more recent times, the great innovators of the computer industry have brought positive changes into the lives of millions with their new products and made fortunes doing so. Rand emphasizes that the greatest capitalists are entrepreneurs with new ideas. In a free country, where Rearden and Dagny would have the liberty to promote this innovation, Rearden Metal would revolutionize industry, improve the general quality of life, and earn millions for Hank Rearden.

Unfortunately, Dagny and Rearden do not live in a free country. The government holds the premise that individuals must sacrifice themselves for the public welfare. When individuals do not volunteer that sacrifice, the state has the legal power to force them to do so. This premise robs Rearden of his ore mines using the justification that Rearden is already successful, so someone less successful should be given a chance. Furthermore, because Rearden intends to sell his metal on the open market, he poses a threat to the State Science Institute. In the government's view, he is dangerous to the "public welfare." The Institute's response is a smear campaign based on fabricated allegations regarding hypothetical problems with Rearden Metal. The unjust campaign is designed to hinder Rearden's success, weakening him until he agrees to obey the Institute's wishes. The rulers aren't interested in promoting the metal's benefits to raise the standard of living. Instead, they're interested in increasing their political power. Ayn Rand shows that in a socialist system, the government violates the rights of the most productive people. As a result, the economy suffers.

Theme

The title of this chapter employs the terminology of Karl Marx to promote an opposite meaning. Marx, the founder of communism, held that in a capitalist system, the wealthy oppress the poor. Rand, a defender of capitalism, shows that in a socialist or communist system, the government oppresses the productive. This chapter raises the question, "Who—and in which system—exploits whom?" In a purely capitalist system, Rearden and Dagny create superb products and services that benefit customers and provide employment for workers. Rand argues that with pure capitalism, the exploitation Marx describes does not exist. But in a socialist system, the government uses its power to shackle and stifle people like Rearden and Dagny. The socialist politicians, while relying on and benefiting from the great productiveness of Rearden and Dagny, enact legislation and policies that make it impossible for Rearden and Dagny to produce.

Part One
Chapter 8—The John Galt Line

Summary

Rearden sells his ore mines to Paul Larkin and his coal mines to Ken Danagger, a hard-bitten Pennsylvania coal producer who started his career as a miner. Rearden's calls to Wesley Mouch in Washington go unanswered, and he then receives a letter announcing Mouch's resignation. Two weeks later, Rearden reads in the newspapers that Mouch has been appointed Assistant Coordinator of the Bureau of Economic Planning and National Resources.

Meanwhile, despite concerted public and government opposition, Dagny completes construction of the John Galt Line on time. She asks for volunteers among Taggart employees to run the first train, and she receives offers from virtually every engineer on the system. The volunteers draw lots for the run and, at a press conference, Dagny and Rearden announce that they'll ride in the cab of the engine on the new line's first train run. Although many people predict that the rail will crack and the bridge will collapse, the first run of the John Galt Line is a resounding success. Afterward, Dagny and Rearden have dinner privately with Ellis Wyatt at his home. When dinner is over and it's time to retire, Dagny and Rearden make love for the first time.

Commentary

Rearden doesn't realize that Paul Larkin is part of the corrupt deal brokered by James Taggart and Orren Boyle that is designed to strip him of his mines and extinguish the Phoenix-Durango Railroad. Rearden sells his mines to Larkin because he thinks he's trustworthy, but Larkin is another corrupt businessman who prospers only in a socialist system. However, Rearden does have a trustworthy ally in Ken Danagger. Danagger is a self-made man. He started at the bottom of the coal business as a miner and rose to the top by means of his own ability and indomitable work ethic, like Rearden. As men who make their own way in the world, relying neither on handouts nor government coercion, Danagger and Rearden understand each other.

The actions of Wesley Mouch are, of course, those of a corrupt politician. His betrayal of Rearden and his affiliation with the James Taggart camp are examples of a socialist economy at work. When the government is granted the legal power to control the economy, it has the power to dispense economic favors. A government with such power attracts power-seeking politicians as well as corrupt, incompetent businesspeople who flourish only behind the barrel of the government's gun. Mouch, for example, is an inconsequential nobody. In a capitalist system, where he would have to compete fairly on an open market, he would not succeed. But in a socialist system, where he can manipulate the coercive power of the state, Mouch can rise to a position of influence in the government.

Character Insight

The events surrounding the completion and running of the first train on the John Galt Line are significant for their portrayal of two contrasting cognitive camps. James Taggart and others are concerned because public opinion is firmly set against Rearden Metal and Dagny's railroad. In fact, Jim tries to buy steel rail from the Phoenix-Durango line, which is closing. Although such a purchase would be costly, Jim says that the goodwill generated by caving in to public demand would more than compensate the railroad's expense. On the other hand, Dagny and Rearden are utterly unconcerned that public opinion is against them, because they know that they have a vastly more powerful ally—the facts. Rearden Metal is superb, and the facts will speak for themselves.

Theme

Through the characters of James Taggart and other parasitic people, Ayn Rand dramatizes the theory that truth is defined by social opinion—that "fifty million Frenchmen can't be wrong," that cognition is a democratic process, and that truth is determined by vote. Through the characters of Dagny and Rearden, Rand exemplifies the theory that truth results when an idea corresponds to facts—that a Rearden Metal bridge will stand or fall based on its molecular properties, not on public opinion. Dagny and Rearden are rational and scientific, relying on facts. James Taggart looks to public opinion for the truth, much like a poll-dependent politician. In a way, the fact that Dagny and Rearden pay no attention to mistaken public opinion is a sign of respect for their fellow man; they are confident that most people are rational enough to accept the truth when they see it for themselves. Dagny and Rearden believe that when the John Galt Line runs successfully, the public will be convinced of the fact that Rearden Metal is superior to any other metal. They believe that the public will ignore the corrupt information they've been fed by government agencies.

The relationship growing between Rearden and Dagny is based on the profound values that they share. Their mutual love of industrialization, technological advance, and man's prosperity on earth goes beyond the immediate commitment that they both have to the Rearden Metal track and the John Galt Line. Likewise, the cognitive method described above—the commitment to facts and the rejection of social opinions—is their deepest connection. Given the principles that they share and the battle that they fight to defend those principles, it is inevitable that Dagny and Rearden fall in love.

Part One
Chapter 9—The Sacred and the Profane

Summary

The morning after their night of passionate lovemaking, Rearden is angry. He regards sex as a low impulse of the flesh, and he feels contemptuous of Dagny (and especially himself) for craving "obscene" pleasures. Dagny rejects his scorn, because she regards sex with Rearden as noble—something to be proud of. She tells him joyously that she makes no other claims on him but this: When he seeks to satisfy this "lowest" of his bodily urges, he must bring his urges to her.

James Taggart meets an innocent shop girl who is star-struck by his fame. Cherryl Brooks came from a poor family and moved to New York because she wanted more from life. She admires achievement and believes that Jim—along with Dagny and Rearden—is responsible for the success of the John Galt Line. Taggart takes a perverse pleasure in her misguided hero worship. Around this time, Taggart's flunky, Wesley Mouch, is appointed Top Coordinator of the Bureau of Economic Planning and National Resources.

Dagny and Rearden take a vacation together, driving through the countryside. In Wisconsin, they visit the former site of the Twentieth Century Motor Company, looking for machine tools. In the research lab of the factory, they find the abandoned remnant of a motor that was designed to take static electricity from the atmosphere and convert it into usable energy. They're shaken to find a motor that would have revolutionized industrial production lying rejected on a scrap heap. Dagny and Rearden are determined to find the inventor.

Commentary

Theme

The differences between the ways Rearden and Dagny view sex are indicative of an underlying philosophical difference. Rearden recognizes that the mind and its achievements are noble, but he believes that the desires of the body are low and base. Although he's generally a rational man, he holds what Rand portrays as an irrational viewpoint regarding the relative value of mind and body. Many philosophies and religions teach that only the mind or soul is pure; the body and its urges are ignoble. Dagny utterly rejects this mind-body dichotomy. She realizes that she's specifically attracted to Rearden because of the enormity of his achievements. She loves and desires him because of his intellectual and moral greatness. She also realizes that Rearden is similarly attracted to her because of her own accomplishments, although Rearden himself doesn't yet recognize this truth. Dagny repudiates the split between mind and body because she recognizes that, for a rational man, the desires of the body flow logically from the understanding and evaluations of the mind.

Character Insight

The beginning of the romance between James Taggart and Cherryl Brooks is motivated by opposite premises. Cherryl is a hero worshipper who sincerely admires great achievement and who mistakenly believes that Taggart is one of the great men responsible for the triumph of the John Galt Line. Taggart, on the other hand, is a *nihilist*, a person who hates achievements and the great people who create them. He attempts to defeat Dagny and Rearden because of their ability, and he hates Francisco d'Anconia because of his genius. The great men are too powerful for him to destroy, but he can take his revenge on the little hero worshipper who admires them. This is his motivation for his relationship with Cherryl.

The discovery of the motor is a major turning point in the novel's plot. Prior to the discovery, Dagny's primary goal was to build the John Galt Line (which is now, once again, the Rio Norte Line of Taggart Transcontinental). Now, she shifts her energies to discovering the secret of the motor. Dagny understands that this invention will do much more than save her railroad; it will transform every aspect of man's life on earth in a more powerful way than the invention of the electric light. Therefore, she's understandably desperate to find the inventor. In addition, the discovery of the motor adds to the mystery that lies at the center of the novel's plot. How could such an extraordinary device be left unrecognized on a scrap heap? Dagny is determined to find the answer, as well as the inventor.

Part One
Chapter 10—Wyatt's Torch

Summary

Dagny begins the search for the motor's inventor, interviewing the town officials in Rome, Wisconsin where the Twentieth Century Motor Company was located. But when she contacts her assistant Eddie, he warns her that the politicians are threatening to pass laws that would kill industrial production in Colorado. The Union of Locomotive Engineers demands that the maximum speed for all trains on the Rio Norte Line be reduced to 60 miles per hour, and the Union of Railway Conductors and Brakemen demands that the length of all trains on the line be reduced to 60 cars. Likewise, the states of Wyoming, New Mexico, Utah, and Arizona demand that no more trains run in Colorado than in any of these neighboring states. A group headed by Orren Boyle demands the passage of a Preservation of Livelihood Law, which would limit the production of Rearden Metal, and other businessmen demand passage of a Fair Share Law, which would give an equal amount of Rearden Metal to any customer who wants it.

In the meantime, Rearden has lost his supply of iron ore. Paul Larkin, in compliance with the terms of the crooked deal that James Taggart arranged, sold the ore to Orren Boyle and shipped it via Taggart's railroad rather than the cheaper lake ore boats.

Dagny's search for the inventor of the motor leads her to the widow of William Hastings, former chief engineer at the Twentieth Century Motor Company. Mrs. Hastings tells Dagny that one of her husband's young assistants was the motor's inventor. She doesn't know his name, but she's met a man who was a mutual friend of her husband and the inventor. Mrs. Hastings directs Dagny to a remote diner in the mountains of Wyoming, and Dagny goes to visit. The man working as a cook knows the inventor, but he refuses to give Dagny any information. Dagny is stunned to learn that the cook is Hugh Akston, the last great philosopher, who retired from his profession many years ago. When she arrives back in Cheyenne, Dagny learns that the socialist rulers have passed a series of directives in accordance with the demands made by the unions, Colorado's neighboring states, and mooching businessmen. A special tax has been levied on Colorado so it can assist its financially needier neighbors. Dagny is terrified at how the defiant Ellis Wyatt will respond. She races to Wyatt's Junction but finds that she's too late. Wyatt has set fire to his wells and disappeared.

Commentary

Theme

This chapter deepens Ayn Rand's portrayal of socialism as parasitical. Rearden, Dagny, and the great Colorado industrialists have, against terrible difficulties, created enormously productive enterprises. They create steel, oil, transportation, and superb innovations. The goods and services they provide make it possible to build and heat homes, construct and fuel automobiles, and participate in countless other productive activities. As a result, they create jobs for thousands of employees. In a capitalist system, the great Colorado industrialists would be free to sell their products to customers and make the fortunes that they've earned. But under socialism, they're forced to carry less competent people along with them. The unions of railroad workers clamor for shorter trains that run at lower speeds, and the government makes these demands law. This means that Taggart Transcontinental must run more trains and hire more men to do the same amount of work. Therefore, in return for her superb work, Dagny is compelled to run an inefficient, costly line that doesn't generate the profit it could. The union membership is rewarded while Dagny, the line's creator, is penalized.

Unfortunately, Rearden's situation is even worse. The government and many businessmen tried to block Rearden from putting Rearden Metal on the market. They threatened him, smeared the reputation of his metal, and robbed him of his ore mines. No one but Dagny had the wisdom and courage to buy his new product. But now that Dagny and Rearden have demonstrated the metal's worth, every one of his enemies demands the metal, and the government forces Rearden to fulfill their demands. Even worse, Rearden's competitors, recognizing the huge demand for the metal, convince the government to limit Rearden's output. Therefore, Rearden must sell to every person or business that wants his product while simultaneously restricting his output. The laws pull Rearden in opposite directions. He is tortured for the enormity of his achievement while men like Boyle, Larkin, and James Taggart benefit. With this scenario, Ayn Rand makes a compelling condemnation of socialism. In forcing the great creators to support those who cannot match their achievements, the socialist government penalizes a man for his ingenuity and hard work and rewards other men for their lack of accomplishment.

Theme

Dagny's relentless quest for the motor's inventor further shows the virtues of freedom. In a capitalist system, Dagny could profit from her recognition of the motor's worth. She would be free to hire the inventor and use his motor to revolutionize the transportation industry. In time, customers would recognize the superiority of the new motor, just as they recognized the great merit of Rearden Metal. Taggart Transcontinental's improved transportation would earn the company—and Dagny—a fortune. But under socialism, Rand argues, the goal is to serve the needy and the unproductive, not to provide justice to the men and women of achievement. Like Rearden and Dagny, the motor's inventor would be enslaved to serve a horde of parasites under a socialist government. Rand's message is that capitalism is the system of justice, because it rewards the good. Socialism, on the other hand, is a system of injustice, because it penalizes the good and rewards unproductive moochers.

Literary Device

This chapter's title refers to the rebelliousness of Ellis Wyatt's independent spirit. Wyatt will not be shackled. Rather than permit his achievement to be looted in order to support the parasites, he destroys it. Wyatt is both a symbol and a warning: He is a symbol of the great creative and free spirit that tyranny can't subjugate and a warning to those who try to enslave him. "Don't tread on me" was a saying popular at the time of the American Revolution, and Wyatt represents that same spirit of freedom. He won't serve people who try to loot his property. In defying them, he delivers a severe blow to their scheme to redistribute wealth.

Part Two
Chapter 1—The Man Who Belonged on Earth

Summary

The economy in Colorado is collapsing. Nobody has been able to replicate Ellis Wyatt's method of creating oil from shale, and without the Wyatt fields, the companies dependent on them go out of business. Andrew Stockton, the Colorado businessman who operates the country's best foundry, makes a fortune because many businesses convert to coal. However, Stockton suddenly retires and vanishes. Shortly after, Lawrence Hammond, another Colorado industrialist and the last great manufacturer of automobiles, also retires. Dagny is compelled to steadily cut trains on the Rio Norte Line.

Dagny calls Dr. Robert Stadler regarding the motor. Realizing that her quest to find the inventor has reached a dead end, she now hopes to find a scientist capable of reconstructing the motor from its remnant. Dr. Stadler looks at the motor and the remaining pages of the explanatory manuscript; he realizes the extraordinary breakthrough in the field of energy that the inventor made. Dr. Stadler is puzzled why such a mind would waste his time making such practical things as motors. He refers Dagny to Quentin Daniels, a promising young physicist at the Utah Institute of Technology, who has refused to accept a government position.

The government makes a ruling regarding the amount of Rearden Metal that Rearden can sell per customer, and the rulers send a bright young man fresh out of college to Rearden's mills to function as Deputy Director of Distribution. The steelworkers call him the "Wet Nurse." The State Science Institute places an order for Rearden Metal, which Rearden refuses to honor. When a representative from the Institute comes to his office, Rearden begins to realize that the socialist looters depend on his moral consent and that he must not give it to them in the future.

Commentary

Character Insight

Although he possesses an extraordinary intellect, Robert Stadler holds a mistaken premise regarding the mind's proper role in human life. Stadler is a brilliant theoretical physicist, but he has contempt for the practical affairs of living. He believes that the mind is effective only when dealing with questions of pure science—issues of abstract speculation—such as the research on the nature of cosmic rays that established his reputation. All questions of practical application involve a human element, and Stadler thinks that men are fundamentally irrational. Stadler believes that most humans are driven by impulses and desires, not by the mind. His belief about the nature of humanity is the reason why Stadler was instrumental in founding the State Science Institute. He assumes that people won't voluntarily support science and the mind; therefore, the government must dictate such support. In his view, the ignorant public desires nothing but clever "gadgets" from science—inventions to improve their quality of life. He despises that the public has no regard for the higher concerns of "pure science." He expresses to Dagny his scornful bewilderment that a genius capable of solving the monumental problems of theoretical physics would waste his brains on such a practical device as a motor.

Theme

Dagny's response, however, comes from opposite premises. She knows that the motor's inventor applied his mind to the project "because he liked living on this earth." Dagny rejects the premise that reason is valid only when grappling with a "higher" realm of ideas. She understands that creating prosperity on earth is vital. She knows the role intellect played in Rearden's creation of his metal, in her own achievement of building the John Galt Line, and in the inventor's construction of the motor. She recognizes that, although people may often behave irrationally, their survival depends on embracing their rational nature. In time, the public will recognize facts and understand the truth, just as it has come to see the merits of Rearden Metal and the John Galt Line. Humans must be free to use their own minds. Dagny's estimate of man's nature is significantly different than Dr. Stadler's. He believes that mankind is composed predominantly of irrational brutes, but she knows that man is a rational animal.

Dr. Stadler believes in the mind-body dichotomy much like Rearden, although Stadler holds a different form of the belief. The mind, Stadler believes, has its own "higher" realm of theoretical ideas that only the great scientists and mathematicians understand. The body and its animalistic urges rule the "lower" world, and the mind is powerless to control the body and its urges. Dagny understands that Stadler's ideas are mistaken. She argues that the mind is the power that makes man's life on earth possible. Dagny rejects the mind-body dichotomy, believing instead in mind-body integration.

Theme

Rearden's growing realization that evil men require some moral consent from their victims—and that the victims must, as their fundamental means of self-protection, withhold such consent—is crucial. As Rearden understands his seminal insight more fully in subsequent chapters, he'll be better able to defend himself against his enemies.

Glossary

pure, abstract science theoretical studies in math and physics that do not relate directly to the development of practical technologies.

sanction something, such as a moral principle or influence, that makes a rule of conduct or a law binding. Rearden begins to realize that the looters need some type of moral permission from Dagny and himself and that, more broadly, evil men require moral permission from their victims. What the exact nature of this sanction is, he doesn't yet know.

Part Two
Chapter 2—The Aristocracy of Pull

Summary

Dagny looks at the list of the great Colorado industrialists who have vanished and suspects the existence of a destroyer. She starts to believe that someone is systematically removing the country's most productive minds. She can only shake her head in despair at the collapse of industry in Colorado. Rearden, meanwhile, secretly sells a larger amount of Rearden Metal than is legally permitted to Ken Danagger.

James Taggart marries the innocent shop girl Cherryl Brooks. Because his wife requests that he do so and he feels obligated to respect her wishes, Rearden attends the wedding. Francisco d'Anconia arrives and tells Taggart that he's grateful for the political deal that Taggart and his socialist colleagues brokered months ago that is putting American producers of copper out of business. The deal makes d'Anconia Copper (in which Jim and his friends hold a large amount of stock) virtually the sole copper producer on earth.

When someone makes a remark claiming that Francisco is a depraved product of money, Francisco responds with a brilliant speech that praises the virtue of wealth. Rearden is drawn to Francisco and the liberating power of his ideas, but he expresses contempt for the way in which Francisco has profited from the legal destruction of his competitors. Francisco tells Rearden of the fires and cave-ins that, though causing no injuries, will imminently wipe out a part of d'Anconia Copper. Francisco also announces his company's problems to the entire room, causing panic for James Taggart and the other corrupt investors who now realize that they've lost their money.

Commentary

Theme

Francisco's "money speech" presents the antithesis of the conventional viewpoint that "money is the root of all evil." He points out that money is a tool of exchange, which presupposes productive men and their activities. The production of goods and services is what makes man's life on earth possible. If human survival and prosperity is good, production is profoundly moral. Furthermore, productive effort is fundamentally an intellectual process. Thinkers invent new goods and methods that promote progress, and Rearden is a prime example.

Francisco explains that money is a claim on goods and services, and the goods and services must be *created*. The creative acts of growing food, manufacturing steel, producing oil, or running a railroad give money its meaning and value. The money that a man earns is the symbol of his productive ability and, consequently, his badge of moral honor. Money, because of the exacting demands it makes on a man's productive effort and its role as the medium of exchange for the goods and services created, must be considered the root of all good, Francisco states. Money makes man's life on earth possible.

Francisco presents his ideas on money primarily to Rearden. For his own purpose, which he will not divulge, Francisco seeks to provide Rearden with an understanding of Rearden's own moral greatness. Rearden currently accepts two mistaken ideas. One is that industrial production is an unspiritual endeavor. The other is that materialistic concerns are immoral, because only purely spiritual activities have moral value. Because of these errors, Rearden can't yet see his own towering stature. He doesn't recognize the intellectual and spiritual component of his steel-making enterprise, nor does he understand the great virtue of his life-giving productivity. Francisco intends to liberate Rearden from his errors and their harmful consequences in his life.

Dagny's suspicion that someone is deliberately luring away the world's greatest minds is significant to the plot. If her assumption is correct, the novel's mystery deepens dramatically. Who is this creature? What possible reason can he, she, or it have for perpetrating such destructive acts? For Dagny, answering these questions is crucial to the survival of her railroad and industrial civilization as a whole.

Glossary

aristocracy of pull a new group of powerful men who have reached their status not by means of talent or initiative, but by means of political connections. In this chapter, it refers to men like James Taggart and his friends, who seek success by currying favor with the politicians in Washington.

Part Two
Chapter 3—White Blackmail

Summary

After the Taggart wedding celebration, Lillian discovers that Rearden has a mistress, but she doesn't know who it is. Rearden realizes that Lillian intends to use his guilt as a means to control him. Dr. Ferris of the State Science Institute comes to Rearden's office and tells him that if he doesn't agree to sell Rearden Metal to the Institute, the government will put him on trial for selling an illegal amount of Rearden Metal to Ken Danagger. Rearden refuses to comply, and he and Danagger are indicted and will go to trial.

Eddie Willers tells the nameless worker in the Taggart cafeteria that Dagny worries about Danagger and that she believes there is a destroyer loose whose purpose is to drain the world's brains. She also believes that Danagger is ready—that he'll be the next to disappear. Eddie tells the worker that Dagny will see Danagger tomorrow, because she's desperate to reach him before the destroyer does. The next day, Dagny reaches Danagger too late. He has just seen a visitor and tells Dagny that he is retiring, but he'll say nothing more.

Francisco comes to Rearden's mills. He says that Rearden is guilty of only one thing: accepting moral condemnation for his virtues. Despite his brilliant work, Rearden has made no profit on Rearden Metal, while vicious connivers like Orren Boyle and his socialist pals received a fortune. Rearden's struggle to produce is met by every type of injustice, and he gets nothing for his effort. Only his tormentors benefit. Francisco mentions Atlas, the titan of Greek mythology who holds up the world. Francisco asks Rearden what he would say if he saw Atlas drained of strength, supporting the globe with the last of his energy, and gasping in pain. Rearden turns the question back to Francisco. Francisco says that he would tell Atlas to shrug. Francisco begins to ask Rearden what could make the suffering he has experienced worthwhile, but the alarm of a mill emergency interrupts him. The two fight a furnace breakout superlatively. When they're finished, Rearden asks Francisco to complete his question, but he won't. Francisco just learned the answer.

Commentary

Francisco's discussion of Atlas is the title scene of the book. The discussion occurs in a context in which Rearden is blackmailed and indicted for his "crime" of carrying the country on his back. Rearden and Dagny are the last productive giants left in the world. The rest have been stifled and/or have disappeared. Without Rearden, the economy will collapse. He is the Atlas holding up the country's economic system. In return for his prodigious effort and life-giving achievements, he is morally condemned, robbed, harassed, threatened, blackmailed, and accused of criminal wrongdoing.

Francisco points out the terrible injustice that Rearden accepts—the injustice of the superbly virtuous man who carries a horde of vicious looters and permits them to set the moral terms. What if Atlas should throw the world off his shoulders and refuse to sacrifice his life for a world that victimizes him? What does this analogy mean for Rearden? Before Francisco can ask a more pointed question, the men are interrupted by the emergency of a furnace breakout. When the two have successfully combated it, Francisco backs away from their previous discussion. He knows that Rearden's ability to take joyous action in service of what he loves enables him to bear the heavy injustices. Nevertheless, Francisco's unasked question still hangs in the air. What will Rearden do when he's so shackled by the looters' controls that he can no longer serve his own values?

The other major event of this chapter is Dagny's realization that the retirement and disappearance of the world's great producers is not a series of unconnected occurrences. A conscious purpose ties the disappearances together—some diabolical plan to remove from the country its greatest minds. Dagny names the person or thing responsible the "destroyer." When she speaks to Ken Danagger, who announces his retirement based on his meeting with a mysterious visitor, Dagny's suspicions are confirmed. The questions raised here are of monumental importance. Who is the destroyer and what is his/her intent? Who is the nameless worker to whom Eddie Willers confides the railroad's secrets, and is he related to the destroyer's activities? What is Francisco's purpose in seeking the moral liberation of Hank Rearden? Dagny's search for answers will determine the future of industrial civilization.

Part Two
Chapter 4—The Sanction of the Victim

Summary

The night before Rearden's trial, he finally confronts his worthless brother. Rearden says that his brother's fate is no longer his concern. He realizes that for years, his silent consent has enabled his family to endlessly inflict injustice on him. Rearden, the victim, now withdraws his sanction. He'll no longer accept his family's moral standards or their condemnations.

At his trial, Rearden refuses to recognize the court's right to try him. He doesn't regard his sale to Ken Dannager as a crime, and therefore he volunteers no defense. He states that he's proud of every penny he has earned by means of his productive effort in competition on an open market. He knows that he has committed no crime. Rearden Metal is his invention; morally, he has the right to sell as much of it as he pleases. He's being tried on charges that violate his rights and leave him no grounds on which to rationally defend himself. Therefore, he refuses to attempt a defense. He refuses to participate in a charade that makes it look like he has rights. The crowd agrees with Rearden, and the judges decide to fine him and suspend the sentence.

Rearden goes to visit Francisco d'Anconia at his hotel suite in New York. In expressing his admiration for Francisco's intellect, he asks how Francisco can waste his extraordinary talents on a promiscuous hedonism. Francisco responds by discussing the meaning of sex. Francisco says that, regardless of the image he has publicly cultivated, he has slept with only one woman in his life. Rearden believes him. Rearden tells Francisco that he ordered a supply of copper from d'Anconia Copper for a supremely important customer (Taggart Transcontinental), and Francisco is stunned. He reaches for the phone but stops, and Rearden senses that Francisco has the power to prevent some action from transpiring but won't. Francisco swears to Rearden by the woman he loves that he is Rearden's friend. However, several days later, when Rearden learns that Ragnar Danneskjöld sunk the ships bearing his supply of copper, he knows that he must avoid Francisco or he'll kill him on sight.

Commentary

Theme

In this chapter, Rearden withdraws his moral sanction from both the family and the politicians that persecute him. He has realized that morality is the most powerful weapon that evil men wield in their war against good. ("They have a weapon against you," Francisco said at Rearden's wedding anniversary. "Ask yourself what it is, sometime.") The self-sacrifice moral code has been used against him for years. The self-sacrifice moral code allows worthless men to make outrageous demands of productive men, who feel morally obligated to satisfy them. Under this code, a productive man supports a gang of parasites, martyring himself in the name of selfless service. He must embrace his exploiters and proclaim his duty to them. He must feed them his lifeblood while accepting their sneers, abuse, and condemnation. The good man is forced to sanction his self-immolation.

Theme

In *Atlas Shrugged*, Ayn Rand asks what would happen if productive men rejected the demands for service to the parasites and refused to accept guilt for their achievements. Rand provides the answer through Rearden's transformation. Rearden has come to understand that his productiveness is a great virtue and that the behavior of his family and the politicians is evil. At his trial, Rearden refuses to accept their moral right to loot his wealth. By withdrawing his tolerance of their actions, he exposes them for what they are—thieves with vicious pretensions to moral rectitude.

Francisco's sex speech furthers Rearden's liberation from the ethical system that has constrained him for so long. Rearden mistakenly believes that bodily desires are divorced from intellect and the soul. At some level, Rearden knows that his attraction to Dagny is more than physical. His body wants her because his mind knows her greatness. While consciously holding the philosophy that divides the mind from the body, he holds an inner belief—and lives by the view—that the two support each other. Francisco merely gives him the words to recognize what he has always known was true.

Part Two
Chapter 5—Account Overdrawn

Summary

The United States has no more copper producers. d'Anconia Copper is the last producer on earth, but none of its ships can reach America because Ragnar Danneskjöld sinks them. Consequently, no more electric appliances are being manufactured in the United States.

Rearden Steel experiences the first failure in its history. Because he cannot get copper, Rearden can't deliver the Rearden Metal rail for Taggart Transcontinental's disintegrating mainline track. As a result, Taggart Transcontinental's track crumbles, train wrecks proliferate, and shippers go out of business. Virtually no important shippers remain on the Rio Norte Line, and the formerly booming industrial towns in Colorado are now destitute. Finally, Dagny is forced to close that line.

James Taggart finds himself squeezed from all sides by the demands of his company and various groups that seek to profit from it. Taggart seeks a raise in shipping rates to keep his company afloat, but the shippers demand a rate reduction. The railroad unions demand a wage increase, and the government grants Taggart Transcontinental permission to close the Rio Norte Line only in exchange for acceptance of the union's demands. The politicians hold the threat of reduced shipping rates over the railroad's head.

The government is ready to launch a new piece of legislation, and it wants no trouble from Rearden. Taggart knows that if he has valuable information about Rearden, he can trade the information to keep shipping rates steady. Taggart goes to Lillian for help. Lillian discovers that Rearden's mistress is Dagny. When Lillian demands that Rearden give Dagny up, Rearden responds that he would rather see Lillian dead first.

Commentary

Literary Device

In this chapter, Rand shows the cause-and-effect relationships between events in a country's economy. Because the politicians previously choked off American copper producers, Rearden is unable to get copper when Ragnar Danneskjöld prevents Francisco's ships from reaching American ports. Because Rearden cannot procure copper—and because he is prohibited by the Equalization of Opportunity law from mining it himself—he cannot manufacture the Rearden Metal rails needed by Taggart Transcontinental. Because the railroad can't get the new track, it must keep using its decaying track, which causes endless train accidents. Because of poor freight service, shippers are unable to get their goods to market, and some go out of business. As a result of business shutdowns, there is no longer freight traffic on the John Galt Line and Dagny must close it, ripping up the track to support the transcontinental line. The events of this chapter provide a powerful indictment of the results of a country's shift from a capitalist economy to a socialist one.

Theme

Augmenting this indictment is the inevitable corruption surrounding the government's seizure of power. When private individuals aren't free to set shipping costs and wage rates, the operation of the law of supply and demand is suspended. Taggart Transcontinental isn't free to charge the shipping rates it requires to make a profit, and manufacturers aren't free to ship by another railroad if it deems Taggart Transcontinental's rates too high. Similarly, companies are not free to offer wage rates based on the value of labor, and workers aren't free to accept or reject the proffered wage. When the government takes over an economic system, it determines such prices and rates by decree. The government attracts to itself the kind of power-seeking politicians who desire to rule men's lives, and it then finds itself in the midst of a life-and-death struggle involving warring pressure groups. The railroads, shippers, and unions all clamor for contradictory measures, and the government dispenses favors to whichever group has the most influence, friends, votes, or pull at that moment.

When the government controls an economy, the buying and selling of economic favors becomes a logical inevitability. For example, to spring the next series of controls on Rearden, the politicians need to ensure that he doesn't act "disruptively," like he did at his trial. Therefore, the politicians go to James Taggart, believing that Rearden's presence at his wedding celebration indicates that Taggart has some degree of influence over him. Taggart, needing some dirt on Rearden to trade to the politicians so they won't lower shipping rates, goes to Lillian, who discovers that her husband's mistress is Dagny Taggart. When Lillian turns this information over to Taggart, he has ammunition to use against the shippers in the ongoing battle to curry favor with the politicians.

Because socialism makes man's survival contingent not on production but on influence, it necessarily breeds significant political corruption.

Glossary

Prometheus *Gr. Myth.* a Titan who steals fire from heaven for the benefit of mankind: in punishment, Zeus chains him to a rock where a vulture (or eagle) comes each day to eat his liver, which grows back each night. In this chapter, Francisco refers metaphorically to John Galt, meaning that the great businessmen brought prosperity to man and have been punished with moral condemnation and strangling laws. Consequently, the great businessmen have retired and withdrawn their benefits until the day when men withhold their punishment.

Part Two
Chapter 6—Miracle Metal

Summary

A group of Washington men that includes James Taggart, Orren Boyle, Wesley Mouch, Dr. Floyd Ferris, and Mr. Thompson (the Head of State) meet to discuss the ramifications of a proposed series of laws that would restrict economic change. Although worried about public backlash, the group decides to enact the laws, which are labeled Directive 10-289. The purpose of Directive 10-289 is to arrest the country's economic decline by freezing the economy in its current state. The directive makes it illegal for workers to leave their current jobs and prevents businessmen from closing their doors. It forbids the introduction of inventions or new products, and it requires companies to produce an amount of annual goods identical to the amount produced the previous year. All wages, prices, profits, and dividends are frozen, and every individual is obligated to spend as much as he did in the previous year. The directive also sets up a Unification Board to hear all disagreements arising from the new laws. The Unification Board's decisions on any issues that surface will be final.

Upon hearing that the directive has been enacted, Dagny immediately resigns, as do other people around the country who refuse to work either as a slave or a slave driver. Dagny retires to a hunting lodge in the mountains that she inherited from her father.

The directive also requires that all patents, including the one for Rearden Metal, be signed over to the government within two weeks. At the end of the two-week period, Rearden hasn't yet complied. Dr. Ferris comes to Rearden's office and tells him that if he doesn't sign, his affair with Dagny will be broadcast to the country, portraying Dagny as a slut. Rearden knows that if Dagny were present, she would not permit him to sign over the rights to his metal. But he also realizes the magnitude of his guilt. He knows that he should have immediately divorced Lillian and proclaimed to the world his love for Dagny. He can't allow Dagny to pay the price of his error, so he signs.

Commentary

Directive 10-289 ends economic and personal freedom in the United States. The government now controls every aspect of an individual's economic life; it is a dictatorship. The best minds, including Dagny's, can't tolerate this change and choose to retreat.

But while the directive itself has an astounding impact, the most important event of this chapter is the steadily increasing liberation of Hank Rearden from the looters' moral code. Rearden has finally realized that he follows the code of life. He can mine ore, manufacture steel, create Rearden Metal, earn a fortune, make love to Dagny, and, in countless other ways, exult in his ability to live. Lillian and her allies can do none of these things. They can't produce steel or anything else. In fact, they couldn't even conceive of something as valuable as Rearden Metal. They are incapable of true love, and to them "friendship" denotes not affection and respect, but the opposite: mutual contempt and a desire to use each other to attain corrupt ends.

People such as Lillian, James Taggart, Wesley Mouch, and all the other looters can't survive on their own, and the purpose of the current government policies is to ensure that creative, productive people can't survive either. If Rearden's is the code of life, the government's is the code of death. He now understands the one error he's made—and its importance. He accepted the moral code of self-sacrifice, which convinced him that he had a duty to submit to suffering at the hands of Lillian, his family, and the politicians. By doing so, Rearden betrayed the code of life by which he's always lived, and he put his incomparable virtue in service to the code of death. He has made an enormous, though innocent, error, and he knows that he must pay for it, not Dagny. This is why he signs away the rights to Rearden Metal. He is now free forever from the code of death that has caused him so much undue suffering.

Glossary

company union an organization of workers in a single company, not affiliated with any group of labor unions. The term generally implies control by the employers. In this novel, the term refers to the Rearden Steel Workers Union. Because Rearden demands the best labor force, he pays wages significantly higher than any union scale in the country.

Part Two
Chapter 7—The Moratorium on Brains

Summary

Eddie Willers tells the worker in the Taggart cafeteria that Dagny has resigned and is staying at her lodge in the Berkshires. The worker mentions to Eddie that every year he takes a month off at his own expense to spend with friends.

Hank Rearden moves out of his house and gets an apartment in Philadelphia. Knowing that the looters' knowledge regarding his relationship with Dagny came from Lillian, he instructs his lawyer to do whatever is necessary to obtain a divorce devoid of alimony or property settlement. Walking to his apartment one night from the mills, he is approached by a stranger who wants to give Rearden money in the form of gold bars. The stranger explains that the gold is a partial repayment for the income taxes that Rearden has paid for years. The stranger says that he can't stand the injustice of the looters robbing Rearden of his metal. Rearden is at first appalled to learn that the man is the pirate Ragnar Danneskjöld, yet just moments later, he lies to the police to prevent Danneskjöld's capture.

The Taggart Comet breaks down in the mountains of Colorado, stranding a train full of passengers. Replacement diesel engines aren't available, only a coal burner that isn't safe to navigate through the lengthy tunnel on the Comet's route. Kip Chalmers, a prominent politician riding the Comet on his way to a rally in San Francisco, bullies the railroad employees into bringing the coal-burning engine despite the risks involved. The coal burner is attached, and the worst possible result occurs: Passengers and crew are asphyxiated in the tunnel. An army munitions train, running off its normal schedule, slams into the stalled Comet in the tunnel. Its armament detonates, bringing tons of mountainside down on the Taggart Tunnel.

Commentary

Character Insight

Ragnar Danneskjöld tells Rearden that he's out to destroy Robin Hood, the man who, according to legend, stole from the rich and gave to the poor. Ragnar, by contrast, steals from the poor to give to the rich. To be exact, he steals from the parasites to give goods back to the men who produced them. Ragnar seizes U.S. relief vessels bound for various Peoples' States around the globe and converts the pirated goods into gold for men like Rearden.

Literary Device

Ragnar is a powerful force for justice in the story. He risks his life every day in his battle to ensure that looters don't benefit from the goods they extort and that productive men receive restitution. His character embodies irony; in order to fight for justice, he's compelled to become a criminal. After talking with Ragnar, Rearden starts to understand that when the law is engaged in robbery, people who want to return stolen goods to their rightful owners must become outlaws.

The Taggart Tunnel disaster is brought about by factors much deeper than politics. The best minds—especially Dagny's—have resigned from the railroad because it's impossible to produce under the arbitrary decrees of the looters' regime. Their unswerving commitment to facts, no matter how unpleasant, is what makes minds such as Dagny's the best. However, this rational perspective is exactly what the railroad currently lacks. Under Dagny's watch, the whims of a powerful politician wouldn't warrant consideration above the facts. Dagny would've refused to allow a coal burner to enter the tunnel, and Kip Chalmers would've punished her by using his political influence.

But with Jim Taggart's friends now running the railroad's Operating Department, the situation is different. To Jim's friends, facts are malleable details that can be molded by the caprices of men with political power. The laws of science and nature don't take precedence in their minds; the commands of powerful men do. Opinions—especially the opinions of political leadership—come first. The slogan "perception is reality" captures the essence of minds such as these. Truth is determined by a public opinion poll. Dagny wants to run trains efficiently; Jim's friends wish to curry favor with the politicians. Dagny will avoid tragic accidents; Jim's friend's will avoid blame. To Dagny, the facts required for a safe journey take precedence; to Jim's friends, avoiding the wrath of powerful politicians takes precedence. Dagny's rational mind is desperately missed in this scene. The difference between her method of thinking and the method of those currently in power is the difference between life and death.

Glossary

moratorium any authorized delay or stopping of some specified activity. In this novel, it refers to the rejection of the mind and the rejection of reason that is responsible for the Taggart Tunnel tragedy.

Part Two
Chapter 8—By our Love

Summary

Francisco pays a surprise visit to Dagny's lodge in the mountains. During their conversation, she realizes something that she'd never guessed about him: He's one of the producers who deliberately withdrew his talents from the world. He was one of the earliest people to do so, although he didn't disappear like the others. Francisco tells Dagny that he's been systematically and slowly (to avoid being suspected and stopped) destroying d'Anconia Copper so the looters are left with nothing. He also makes it clear that he still loves Dagny and that she was the hardest thing for him to give up when he made his decision years ago. He urges her to leave the railroad to the looters, because without her it's useless anyway. He pleads with her not to give the looters her mind. But as they talk, the radio broadcasts news of the Taggart Tunnel disaster, and Dagny instinctively races to her car.

Having returned to her office, Dagny restores transcontinental rail traffic by rerouting trains onto the tracks of other rail companies. She makes plans for Taggart Transcontinental to lay its own track around the wreck. She calls Rearden to order new rails. She admits to him that she realizes the looters take advantage of her love for her work and Rearden's love for his. The looters know that people like Dagny and Rearden can't imagine abandoning their work.

Commentary

Character Insight

Part of the mystery at the heart of this story begins to become clear in this chapter. Francisco reveals that he hasn't degenerated into the worthless playboy Dagny had assumed. Instead, he's remained true to the code of production, freedom, and life—in opposition to the code of parasitism, dictatorship, and death—by withdrawing his mind and his products from the looters' world. He refuses to prop up their regime, and he urges Dagny to do the same. The looters depend on minds such as Dagny's. Francisco argues that the producers must not give the looters the benefit of their brains. Without the support of creative minds, the looters' regime will collapse because of its own irrationality. Only then will the rational men be free to rebuild the world. This is the battle that Francisco wages, and he urges Dagny to join.

Dagny's immediate flight back to the railroad upon hearing news of the disaster shows that she's not ready to join Francisco's battle. She is still tied to her love of the railroad. Unlike Francisco, Ellis Wyatt, Andrew Stockton, Ken Danagger, and all the others, Dagny isn't ready to walk away from the thing that's given meaning to her life. Her words to Rearden (that form the chapter's title) contain the essence of the bond Dagny feels to the railroad and Rearden feels to his mills. For the sake of their love, the great producers are willing to endure the torture imposed on them by the dictators in Washington.

Theme

Ayn Rand emphasizes here that industrial production is just as creative as writing a novel or composing a symphony. Industrial production is also fueled by love—love for the creation of material abundance and the positive, constructive act of making possible man's life on earth. Such love isn't to be relinquished lightly, which is why Francisco experienced such torment when he chose to leave and is also why Dagny can't yet join him.

Dagny and Rearden have learned that the collapse of the world's economy isn't caused by random factors or solely by the irrationality of the looters' code. The thinkers have systematically withdrawn their minds from the world, hastening the collapse of the looters' regime. Seemingly notorious figures like Francisco d'Anconia and Ragnar Dannejsköld are, in their own ways, fighting the evil that's currently in power. The tempo of the resistance quickens as each great mind walks away from the world. At this point, it begins to look as if the great minds have a chance to defeat the irrational forces in power. But if the thinkers succeed, what will victory cost Dagny's railroad and Rearden's mills?

Part Two
Chapter 9—The Face Without Pain or Fear or Guilt

Summary

The same evening, Francisco comes to Dagny's apartment in one last effort to convince her to quit the railroad. But Dagny responds that if Taggart Transcontinental is to perish with the looters' system, then she will perish with it. Rearden enters and is furious to see Francisco, whom he believes is guilty of the worst kind of betrayal. Francisco is stunned to find that the woman he loves is sleeping with Rearden. When Rearden realizes that Dagny is the woman Francisco loves, he slaps him. Francisco, calling on the greatest self-control possible, refrains from retaliating. He departs.

Dagny receives a letter from Quentin Daniels informing her that he is resigning. He still wants to solve the secret of the motor, so he will continue to work on rebuilding it privately. But if he succeeds, he will not release the motor for commercial purposes in the looters' world, so he will not accept her money any longer. Dagny, desperate to reach Quentin before the destroyer does, calls him and makes him promise to wait for her. She will take the Comet west to examine the track in Colorado and to speak with Daniels in Utah.

Eddie Willers, in Dagny's apartment taking notes before her departure, observes Rearden's dressing gown in her closet and realizes that they are lovers. Eddie is shaken. After seeing her off, he eats dinner with the worker in the Taggart cafeteria. He remarks to the worker that his face looks as though he's never known pain or fear or guilt. Eddie tells him that Daniels has worked on the motor for a year and that Dagny is going to Utah to prevent the destroyer from getting him. Eddie also reveals that Dagny is Rearden's lover, and the worker rushes away.

Commentary

When Dagny refuses to withdraw her mind from the looters' world, Francisco makes clear to her that they are enemies and that she is never to ask him for money or help for her railroad. He feels certain that without her and Rearden, the looters cannot survive. Ironically, Dagny is propping up the system the thinkers despise; she is Francisco's most dangerous adversary. Although he still loves her, he must find a way to defeat her.

Character Insight

The possibility that Quentin Daniels might give up his work on the motor is intolerable to Dagny. She needs to know that somewhere in the world the human mind still moves forward. If any hope exists for the future, the great achievements of man's mind cannot be abandoned on a scrap heap. Otherwise, all that remains are the looters and the devastation wrought by their policies. Dagny needs one bright spot related to her work to serve as fuel, as motivation, as some quiet knowledge that the human mind still works toward progress. At a literal level, Dagny's quest to reconstruct the motor is an attempt to develop a specific invention of enormous life-giving power. But the quest is also a symbol of an unbreakable commitment to the mind's power to create life and a refusal to surrender this power to the encroaching Dark Age. Dagny, who worships the highest achievements of man's mind and who has suffered as, one by one, the great thinkers abandoned the country, recognizes that Daniels' work is the mind's last stand in the world. She will defend it until her final breath.

In the course of several hours of one evening, three men discover that Dagny is Rearden's lover. First is Francisco, who has made it clear that, despite his playboy image, he has loved only one woman. Second is Eddie, who has never permitted himself to acknowledge his full feelings for Dagny. Third is the unidentified Taggart worker, who has no discernible connection to Dagny. Francisco, though he hopes to win Dagny again after the looters' world collapses, quietly accepts her relationship with Rearden. Eddie, her childhood friend, is confronted with a painful self-discovery: She means much more to him than a close friend and a respected boss. But the reaction of the Taggart worker seems inexplicable. "What's the matter with you?" Eddie cries on observing the worker's response to his news.

Literary Device

This chapter raises many more questions that deepen the mystery Rand is creating. Why does this Taggart track-hand rush off in distress after hearing that Dagny is sleeping with Hank Rearden? Why does this worker, amid all the noble characters in this book, have a face that Eddie describes as never having experienced pain or fear or guilt? Who is this man that Eddie trusts and to whom he confides the railroad's most important information? Is it merely coincidence that Eddie identifies to him the men whom Dagny considers indispensable to the survival of American industrial civilization, and those men retire and disappear shortly after? Why does he ceaselessly pump Eddie for information regarding the railroad but never divulge anything about himself?

The mystery of the disappearing thinkers begins to center on this unnamed man, though neither Dagny nor Eddie is aware of it yet. In this scene, the worker learns that Quentin Daniels has been rebuilding the motor and that Dagny is desperate to save him from the destroyer. It will take Dagny almost a week to reach Utah. We will soon learn whether her fears of the destroyer are justified.

Glossary

Atlantis the legendary island or continent supposed to have existed in the Atlantic west of Gibraltar and to have sunk into the ocean. Here, used to describe the decline of New York City and of American civilization in general. Atlantis is a symbol of the shining ideal that, inexplicably, mankind has lost.

Part Two
Chapter 10—The Sign of the Dollar

Summary

As Dagny rides west on the train, she encounters a hobo sneaking a ride in the vestibule of her car. She invites him in. His name is Jeff Allen, and he once worked for the Twentieth Century Motor Company. He tells her that he and the factory's other employees first phrased the question, "Who is John Galt?" Twelve years earlier, the company owner died and his heirs took over. The new owners put into practice a plan based on the communist slogan, "From each according to his ability, to each according to his need." The plan enslaved the most able to the unable. The first man to quit the company was a young engineer who said that he would put an end to such irrationality once and for all—he said he would stop the motor of the world. Years passed, factories closed, production declined, and the motors stopped. Jeff Allen and the factory's other workers began to wonder if the young engineer had succeeded in his mission. The engineer's name was John Galt.

The train suddenly comes to a stop, and Dagny learns that the crew members have deserted it. Desertion is becoming a common phenomenon, because men are reaching their breaking points and have no legal way to quit their jobs. Many of Taggart's trains have been "frozen" in this way—abandoned on the tracks for someone else to deal with.

Dagny walks down the tracks and phones for help for the abandoned train. She doesn't return to it, however, choosing instead to walk to a small airfield, where she rents a plane. She flies to Afton, Utah, but the airfield attendant tells her that she has just missed Quentin Daniels. He recently left with a man flying a beautiful plane. Dagny knows instinctively that the man flying the plane is the destroyer, and she decides to follow him. She trails him into the most desolate area of the Colorado Rockies and crashes her plane while attempting to follow the destroyer down.

Commentary

The story that the hobo tells about the Twentieth Century Motor Company is important for several reasons. First, Rand uses it to demonstrate the consequences of communism in practice. The primary question raised by a communist system is how an individual's needs can be determined. If a group permits each individual to determine his or her own needs, the group faces the daunting task of having to satisfy every person's desires. The problem is not necessarily that people are unscrupulous; the problem is that in such a case, there is no way to achieve objectivity. Does a man need a car or merely desire it? Does a woman require her house to be painted, or is a new coat of paint desirable but nonessential? Does a man need those books or musical recordings that he loves, which add so much meaning to his life? Who should answer such questions, and by what standard could they judge?

Questions of need cannot be answered objectively. *Need* is a vague and undefinable term in this context. At the Twentieth Century Motor Company, the group voted to decide the needs of each individual, just as the group decided the projected output of each worker based on ability. As a result, each individual was enslaved to the group; his income was determined by his ability to beg rather than by his productive effort. No worker could feel the pride that comes from earning money as a direct result of hard work.

When income is severed from production, incentive necessarily wanes and productivity declines. When the factory's output dropped, the group determined that some people were not working in accordance with their ability. The group sentenced those people to work overtime— without pay, of course, because income is based on need. Not surprisingly, the employees soon started to hate each other and to hide all signs of ability. As a logical consequence, declining production condemned the factory to bankruptcy.

Rand indicates that the worst evil of this communist ideal is that it rewards misery and punishes virtue. It ties a man's income to the number and severity of misfortunes that he and his family experience. It turns his productive ability into a curse, condemning him to ceaselessly toil for the satisfaction of his neighbor's unending desires. The more ability an individual shows, the more he is sentenced to unremitting slavery for the needy, with no gain for his effort. Rand insists that this is the antithesis of a proper moral code, which celebrates the creation of abundance and rewards it by tying income directly to production. Man's life on earth is made possible by virtue of his productivity, not his suffering. Justice and the ability to live successfully require that productive ability be the standard of determining a man's income, not his needs or pain.

The second and more important impact of the story told by Jeff Allen regards John Galt. Dagny now has reason to suspect that there may be a literal John Galt, who is responsible for stopping the motors and draining the brains of the world. If the hobo's story is true, then the destroyer Dagny fears may be this John Galt, who vowed years ago to stop the motor of the world. Dagny has an important clue in her quest to hunt down the destroyer.

Glossary

The sign of the dollar literally stands for a free country's currency. Here, it makes the deeper point that the mind is the faculty responsible for the creation of wealth, and the mind must be free.

Part Three
Chapter 1—Atlantis

Summary

Dagny belly-lands her plane. Her injuries aren't severe, but she does lose consciousness. As she awakens, she looks up at the face of a man kneeling by her side—a face that shows no sign of pain or fear or guilt. The man is John Galt. He is the object of both of Dagny's quests, because he is both the motor's inventor and the destroyer who is draining the brains of the world.

Dagny discovers that all the great minds who retired and vanished from society now live and work in this remote Colorado valley. Ellis Wyatt is here, as are the other Colorado industrialists. Ken Danagger has joined them. The great banker Midas Mulligan owns the valley, and the philosopher Hugh Akston and composer Richard Halley reside here also. Dagny learns, not surprisingly, that Francisco d'Anconia is another thinker who has come here to be free from the looters' oppressive code.

Galt's motor powers the valley's electrical appliances. It also powers a ray screen that shields the valley from view, which is why it remains undiscovered by the outside world. Galt takes Dagny to a building that houses the generator, where she reads his oath inscribed above the door: "I swear by my life and my love of it that I will never live for the sake of another man, nor ask another man to live for mine."

At dinner that night, in the home of Midas Mulligan, Galt quietly tells Dagny the purpose of the valley's residents: They are on strike. The men of the mind refuse to support the looters' system, which consists of involuntary obligations and enforced servitude.

Commentary

Literary Device

The mystery that has compelled much of the novel's plot so far is finally explained in this chapter. The decline of industrial civilization has occurred not solely as a result of the looters' socialist policies. The decline has been hastened by the finest minds in the United States going on strike. The sudden retirements and the disappearance of the country's finest brains now make sense to Dagny (and to the reader). John Galt, the inventor who once worked at the Twentieth Century Motor Company, has kept his word; he is on the verge of stopping the motor of the world by halting invention, production, and all other economic progress.

Theme

Galt was the first person in the group of great minds to understand that the only way rational men can live freely is to withdraw their support of the looters' corrupt code and permit the current economic system to collapse. Only after that happens can the thinkers rebuild the world based on the principles of individual rights and political freedom—on the realization that the human mind must be free. Galt's oath, inscribed over the door leading to the generator, explains the essence of the strikers' code. The strikers are *egoists:* They believe that each individual has an inalienable right to his own life, that a person should pursue his own happiness, and that the individual has no moral obligations to others except to respect their rights to pursue happiness. Galt's oath repudiates the code of *altruism* practiced by the looters, a creed that demands selfless service to others. His oath specifies that an individual must neither sacrifice his values for others nor demand that others sacrifice their values for him.

Galt shared this message with each person now living in the valley, but only when each was prepared to accept his idea. As a result, Galt has orchestrated a strike unlike any other in human history. Obviously, this isn't the first group of people to go on strike while claiming to be indispensable to human well-being. Striking workers have often accused wealthy entrepreneurs and industrialists of exploitation—of gaining profit by robbing the true producer of wealth, the manual laborer. But Galt's strike is designed to show that the mind—not physical labor— is the fundamental source of wealth, and that the men and women who perform intellectual work are the true creators of value. Galt insists that the thinkers—the inventors, innovators, and entrepreneurs who plan a company's long-range policies—are fundamentally responsible for prosperity. Galt intends to prove that when the thinkers participate in the economy, the standard of living is high, but when the thinkers withdraw, the standard of living plummets. The manual laborers stay on the job, and they undeniably do constructive work that aids the production of goods and services. But their work alone, without the guidance of the mind, cannot move the economy forward.

Character
Insight

The reader learns something in this chapter that Dagny doesn't know yet: John Galt works as a laborer for Taggart Transcontinental. He is the nameless worker who pumps Eddie Willers for information in the Taggart cafeteria. We first make this connection when Dagny recognizes the lack of pain, fear, and guilt in his face, because the description matches Eddie's description of the Taggart worker. Galt reveals that he has watched Dagny closely for years, and we now realize from which vantage point.

Part Three
Chapter 2—The Utopia of Greed

Summary

Dagny voluntarily works as Galt's cook and housemaid in the valley. The strikers don't always stay in the valley; they often go to the outside world in order to further their cause. But it's now June, and ever since the valley was established 12 years earlier, the strikers have spent this month at the valley to rest and enjoy time with friends. For the past 12 years, Galt has eaten breakfast on June 1st with his two closest friends: Ragnar Danneskjöld and Francisco d'Anconia. Francisco arrives late this year after desperately seeking the wreckage of Dagny's plane in the mountains. He is overjoyed to find her alive.

Francisco accepts that he has lost Dagny, believing that she now loves Hank Rearden. But Dagny realizes that John Galt is the man that she has looked for all her life. However, she knows that because of his strike, she and Galt stand on opposite sides, and she may never have him. Galt also expresses the depth of his feelings for Dagny, saying that when he first saw her he knew that the abandonment of his motor was not the hardest price he would pay for his strike. He loves her, but he can't touch her because she still works within the looters' system.

Galt knows about the past relationship between Francisco and Dagny and understands that Francisco continues to love her. Dagny fears that Galt may veil his own feelings in order to spare his dearest friend any pain, but Galt refuses to do so, because making such a sacrifice for Francisco would violate his code. Galt requires that Dagny spend a full month in the valley while she decides whether to stay with the strikers or leave. Dagny decides to earn her keep by working as Galt's housemaid during that time. Francisco invites Dagny to stay at his house during the last week of her stay. Dagny puts the decision in Galt's hands, and he declines Francisco's invitation on her behalf.

Although she loves Galt and everything for which the valley stands, at the end of the month, Dagny still believes that there is a chance to defeat the looters and save her railroad, so she decides to return to the outside world. She takes an oath not to reveal the existence of the valley to anyone. Although his friends advise him not to, Galt says that he'll return to the outside world as well, so he can watch Dagny and wait for the day when she decides to join the strike. Galt stipulates that Dagny cannot try to find him and cannot know where he works.

Commentary

Theme

The strikers' valley represents *rational selfishness*, the belief that an individual should pursue the life-enhancing values that promote happiness. To marry Dagny would make Galt happy, but he loves Francisco as well and knows of Francisco's feelings for Dagny. Will Galt sacrifice his feelings for Dagny so Francisco can pursue the woman he loves? For Dagny, the question involves far more than a love relationship. The question involves everything for which Galt, his strike, and the valley stand. Galt's actions remain true to the values that give his life meaning; he refuses to relinquish one moment of his private time with Dagny, not granting to Francisco the chance that he himself desires. Galt's integrity is rock solid. He pursues the love on which his happiness depends, no matter what the circumstances.

Character Insight

Dagny thinks that she has a chance to defeat the looters because she still believes they're rational. Dagny believes that the looters want to live and that they're honestly mistaken in their principles and policies. She thinks that they only need to realize that their altruist ethics, dictatorial politics, and socialist economics are leading to collapse. When the looters see their errors, they'll step back and permit rational producers like Rearden and herself to rebuild the economy. For this reason, Dagny believes that she must return to her railroad.

Galt and the strikers, on the other hand, believe that the looters are irrational—that they're viciously driven by the urge to rule men. The strikers think that the looters see the destructive results of their policies but choose to deny the truth. When reality clashes with their desire to rule and prosper, they evade reality rather than question the desire. They want power regardless of the consequences. Therefore, no amount of evidence that proves the devastating results of their policies will motivate them to change. Galt feels certain that Dagny can't win her battle and wants to be near her when she realizes it too. At this point in the story, the reader is not certain whether Dagny and Rearden are right or whether Galt and the strikers know the truth.

Part Three
Chapter 3—Anti-Greed

Summary

Robert Stadler attends and sanctions a demonstration of the government's previously top secret Project X. The project, housed in rural Iowa, is a new weapon that employs sound waves and is capable of mass destruction. Floyd Ferris convinces Stadler that the weapon is a necessary instrument of control at a time when hysteria and rebelliousness grip the American people.

Dagny returns from the valley to find the railroad in the grip of Washington's latest dictatorial policy: the Railroad Unification Plan. The plan pools all railroad profits together and distributes income based on need rather than production. A gangster named Cuffy Meigs is the Director of Unification.

The looters want Dagny to speak on the radio and reassure the country that the railroad industry isn't disintegrating. Initially, Dagny refuses, but Lillian Rearden visits Dagny and informs her that the rulers know of her affair with Rearden and will announce it publicly if she refuses to make the address. Dagny goes on the radio and speaks openly and proudly about her relationship with Rearden. She states that the government blackmailed Rearden into signing over the rights to his metal. Dagny sees Rearden that night. She cannot tell him where she has been, but Rearden realizes that she met the man she truly loves while she was gone.

Rearden now feels free from the grip of the altruist ethics and yearns to see the man who helped release him—Francisco. Rearden laments that he will never see Francisco again.

Commentary

The Railroad Unification Plan is a desperate ploy that James Taggart and the socialist politicians brokered in an attempt to save Taggart Transcontinental from its own irrational policies. The plan's purpose is to prevent Taggart's bankruptcy by means of feeding off other weaker competitors. For example, because its track was severed by the Colorado tunnel disaster, Taggart Transcontinental uses the transcontinental line of the Atlantic Southern railroad without charge. The competitor pays for the track's upkeep without help from Taggart. Under the Railroad Unification Plan, railroads are paid according to how many miles of track they own rather than how much service they provide. Taggart Transcontinental owns by far the most miles of track (although much of it now sits unused), so Jim's plan ensures that his company gets most of the pooled railroad income. Taggart Transcontinental gets the money while the smaller rail lines go bankrupt. Cuffy Meigs, the director of the plan, is a blatant thief who uses his authority to provide train service to his friends in exchange for a share of their profit.

Dagny refuses to reassure the public about the state of the rail industry because she understands the disastrous long-term consequences of the plan. After the smaller rail lines go bankrupt, nothing can save the larger companies from a similar fate. The looters' policies have strangled industrial production, so the railroads are transporting a mere trickle of freight. The future of the railroad industry is grim, and Dagny wants the public to know the truth. Her broadcast enables her to tell the country the facts regarding the looters' socialist policies.

The broadcast also proves Dagny's pride for her relationship with Rearden and her utter rejection of the mind-body dichotomy. Realizing that their attraction was based on their achievements—on a mutual reverence for the accomplishments of the human mind—Dagny regards Rearden's desire for her as a badge of honor. She proclaims to the world that she has earned the right to sleep with Hank Rearden.

Robert Stadler's acceptance of the horrific Project X is the final destruction of a once great mind. Stadler now openly embraces the rule of brute force. The purpose of the project is to rule by terror a populace that has every right to rebel against the destructive policies of the government. Stadler's endorsement shows that this great mind, which once fought for the freedom of thought, now fights on behalf of a dictatorship.

Glossary

xylophone a musical percussion instrument consisting of a series of wooden bars graduated in length so as to sound the notes of the scale when struck with mallets. In this novel, xylophone is used as a name for a weapon employing sound waves: Project Xylophone. The weapon's purpose is to rule the American people by terror.

epoch-making   an adjective describing an event that ushers in a new historical period. It is used approvingly by Floyd Ferris in this novel to mean the new period in American history introduced by Project X, in which the government will rule the people by brute force.

Part Three
Chapter 4—Anti-Life

Summary

James Taggart wants to celebrate. In several weeks, Argentina will be declared a People's State. Taggart has helped bring to fruition a deal between American, Argentinean, and Chilean politicians, whereby all the holdings of d'Anconia Copper in those South American countries will be nationalized. The politicians have set up a new corporation to manage all the industrial properties of South America. Taggart will sell his shares of d'Anconia Copper and buy stock in the new company, which will earn him a fortune.

However, Cherryl refuses to celebrate such a victory. In the year since her wedding to Jim, she has discovered the truth about him and is tortured by the question of why he married her. Cherryl, disgusted by her husband's desire to break Francisco's spine, leaves their apartment. Later, Lillian Rearden arrives. She pleads with Taggart to use his political pull to prevent her impending divorce from Rearden, which will cut her off without a penny. But Taggart has no power to prevent the divorce. In an attempt to hurt her husband one last time while she is still Mrs. Rearden, Lillian has sex with Taggart.

Cherryl returns home and knows that her husband has been unfaithful. Taggart tells her that he'll never grant her a divorce; he'll use his connections to prevent one, so Cherryl is stuck with him for life. In the ensuing argument, his motive for marrying her becomes clear. Cherryl understands that her husband is a killer who thrives on crippling people's spirits. She races blindly out of their home and into the street. A social worker accosts her and preaches that her despair is caused by selfishness. This encounter is the last straw for Cherryl, who throws herself into the river and drowns.

Commentary

The nature of James Taggart's character is the focus of this chapter. He believes that he'll make a fortune from his latest deal, which will allow him and his political friends to rob Francisco d'Anconia. However, Taggart doesn't want to celebrate the promise of financial gain. He wants to celebrate the blow struck against Francisco—the wound inflicted on a great man. Taggart savors this type of destruction. He has hated Francisco from the earliest days of his childhood. Francisco is a prodigy who excels at every endeavor—physical and intellectual. Jim hates him, not because of any flaw, but because of his joyous, life-giving ability. Jim is riddled with envy, an emotion that Ayn Rand describes as hatred of the good for being good. Taggart recognizes Francisco's genius and nobility of spirit and hates him because of it. For this same reason, he hates Dagny, Ellis Wyatt, and Hank Rearden.

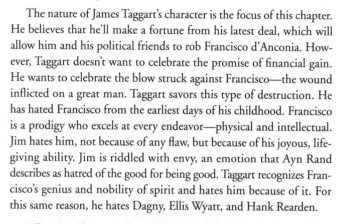

Lillian Rearden resembles Taggart closely. She has only one goal in life: to use guilt, psychological manipulation, and treachery to harm her husband. She wants to hurt him in any way that she can—by criticizing his work and character, by making his home life miserable, by simultaneously refusing him a divorce and forbidding him Dagny, by scheming to rob him of his metal, by aligning herself with the looters, and so on. Like Taggart, she hates Rearden because of his stature. The only reason she has sex with Taggart is to try to hurt her husband. Taggart knows this, and the only words spoken during the act come from Taggart, who calls Lillian "Mrs. Rearden." To wound or disfigure greatness is the desire motivating both characters, but both lack the power to damage Rearden now. Rearden despises Lillian, and her actions no longer affect him. He can defend himself completely against the hatred of such empty souls.

Cherryl is a different story. Unlike Rearden, she is still capable of being hurt by Taggart. Cherryl resembles Eddie Willers in a fundamental way. Both characters have the soul of someone like Dagny or Rearden, but they lack the intellect of such great producers. They understand and worship the achievements of genius, but they can't create Rearden Metal or build the John Galt Line themselves. Cherryl has the pure soul of a hero worshipper. She reveres man at his highest and best. She loves the very greatness that James Taggart seeks to destroy.

Because Taggart has no power to harm Rearden or Dagny, he channels his hatred toward the one person who admired him. With no capacity to defeat the heroes, Taggart takes his revenge by destroying a hero worshipper. Cherryl lacks the intellectual prowess required to defend herself against Taggart, which is the reason he married her. Cherryl is a helpless stand-in for Francisco, Dagny, Rearden, and all the other great people that Taggart hates. Because Taggart's motives are so monstrous, they've remained hidden from Cherryl until now. Before, her purity wouldn't allow her to imagine that such evil exists. When she finally realizes her husband's true nature—and that she is trapped in her marriage—she flees the apartment. However, Cherryl has no place to go because Taggart and his cronies rule the world as well as her home. When the social worker utters the same slogans of self-sacrifice that Taggart and the socialist rulers endorse, Cherryl feels trapped. She senses that she doesn't have a place to go, that the code of evil dominates the globe, and that she'd rather die than exist under such conditions. James Taggart has succeeded in his quest to lash out at those whom he knows to be good.

Part Three
Chapter 5—Their Brothers' Keepers

Summary

Taggart Transcontinental doesn't have copper wire for desperately needed repairs. The copper shortage reaches crisis status when Francisco d'Anconia, on the hour and day that his company is to be nationalized, destroys every mine, piece of property, and bank account belonging to d'Anconia Copper. Nothing remains for the looters to expropriate. Francisco and the elite members of his staff disappear.

Philip and the Wet Nurse both ask Rearden for a job. He rejects Philip because of his incompetence. He says that he would hire the Wet Nurse if possible, but the Unification Board won't permit him to do so. The Wet Nurse warns Rearden that his Washington superiors are planning to spring a new restrictive policy on Rearden, although he doesn't know the details. The looters are slipping their men—thugs, not steelworkers—into Rearden's mills.

The collapse of the economy accelerates under the rule of gangsters such as Cuffy Meigs. He sends thousands of freight cars needed for the Minnesota wheat harvest to a soybean project in Louisiana, which is run by the mother of a Washington politician. The Minnesota crops rot, meaning starvation for many in the coming winter.

One night, an emergency calls Dagny to the Taggart Terminal, where she sees John Galt standing in a group of manual laborers. After she gives the group its orders, she walks into the tunnels, knowing that he'll follow. There, alone in the tunnels under the Terminal Building, Dagny and John Galt make love for the first time. He warns her that he'll lose his life if she inadvertently leads the looters to him.

Commentary

Cuffy Meigs and people like him gain prominence. As the country becomes more fully socialistic, thugs like Cuffy Meigs, whose only goal is to plunder, take control. When the government robs the productive, it also attracts criminals to itself. Dagny realizes that it makes no difference if the railroad's storehouses are raided to support the needy or to bloat the gangsters; either way, the producers are expropriated, making the creation of goods and services impossible. Whether motivated by starvation or exploitation, the welfare workers and the criminals are united in the act of robbing the productive.

Cuffy Meigs sends the Minnesota freight cars to Louisiana because he gets a kickback from the politicians funding the soybean project. If Eugene Lawson, the sniveling former banker, were running the railroad, he would send the cars to Louisiana because the starving people of the blighted southern areas desperately need soybeans. Either way, the wheat growers of Minnesota are abandoned, the railroad is transformed into an instrument of bureaucratic whim, and the citizens are left without grain. When altruism is the dominant moral code, the producers are robbed. Every parasite can join the feeding frenzy.

Literary Device

This chapter's title refers to the biblical story of Cain and Abel. Ayn Rand shows what the religious injunction to be your brother's keeper looks like in practice. Three instances in this chapter embody this injunction. The first instance occurs when the seed grain and the future existence of the Nebraska farmers is seized to feed the starving populace of Sand Creek, Illinois. In this age of enlightenment, says Eugene Lawson, men realize that they are all their brothers' keepers. The second instance occurs when James Taggart, desperate to hold on to the looters' policies that grant him power, begs Dagny to somehow find a way to make the policies work. "Dagny, I'm your brother," he pleads. Despite his role in Cherryl's death, the endless roadblocks he has placed in Dagny's path, and the literal impossibility of making the policies work, he appeals to sibling obligation, hoping to force Dagny into action. The third instance occurs when Philip Rearden, an irresponsible moocher concerned that his gravy train will end if Rearden retires and vanishes, pleads for a job that he can't successfully perform. His brazen request is possible only because he feels justified in arguing that an obligation to one's brother should supersede all other considerations. In all cases, Ayn Rand shows that the unproductive try to argue that an individual is obligated to help either his literal brother or his figurative brothers—humanity. She insists that the motive behind this injunction is to enslave the productive to the moochers, who feel that they have biblical license to take what they want.

Part Three
Chapter 6—The Concerto of Deliverance

Summary

The union of Rearden steelworkers demands a raise, but the Unification Board rejects their demand. A newspaper story claims that the steelworkers are starving and mentions that the raise in wages was rejected. The story doesn't, however, specify who rejected the raise. The government places an order of attachment on all of Rearden's money, so funds aren't available to him. Rearden's family is terrified that he'll retire and vanish. Unconcerned about the impossible burdens that he has to carry, they plead with him to remain.

Rearden goes to New York to meet with Wesley Mouch and several other heads of the looters' regime. They inform Rearden that they'll put a new Steel Unification Plan into effect. Rearden points out that, under the plan, he'll go bankrupt regardless of his output, while Orren Boyle's Associated Steel will receive the bulk of his earnings. He leaves the meeting and drives back to his mills. When he arrives, the mills are under siege. The government thugs placed among his workers have started a riot. They murdered the Wet Nurse when he tried to stop them, and they attack Rearden when he enters the mills. One thug smashes him with a pipe before an unknown worker kills the attacker. When Rearden regains consciousness in the infirmary, he finds that his unknown savior, the same person who organized the workers' defense and defeated the thugs' attack, is Francisco d'Anconia. Francisco has been working as a furnace foreman at Rearden's mills for the two months after he destroyed d'Anconia Copper.

Commentary

The looters organize a systematic attempt to take over Rearden's mills. They know that he won't agree to the Steel Unification Plan. Rearden will reject the plan because it permits Orren Boyle to exist off of his effort while he goes bankrupt. The looters can't afford to lose

Rearden; they're terrified that he'll retire and vanish. Their plan to keep him working is simple. First they attach his funds, so he has no money with which to escape. Second, they threaten his family. If he "deserts" them, his family members will be punished. Not surprisingly, his family begs him to stay. Finally, the looters slip their goons into the mills and stage a riot, supposedly spurred on by Rearden's rejection of a request for wage raises. With violence spiraling out of control at the mills, the looters will step in to protect Rearden's safety by taking over his factory. Francisco's presence quells the riot, defeats the looters' plan and, most important, completes Rearden's liberation from the looters' grip. Rearden is now ready to join the strike. He'll no longer lend his mind to the support of the looters' system.

Rearden believes that his ill-advised slap in Dagny's apartment has cost him Francisco's friendship, but he finds that Francisco loves him too much to let that incident divide them. Francisco understands that, at some implicit level, Rearden has always trusted him. Francisco acted as Rearden's protector from the start. He armed Rearden with the knowledge of his own inestimable moral value. He fought Rearden's enemies for years by destroying his own company and not permitting it to serve those who would torment and enslave Rearden. He brushed off Rearden's insults, understanding that they proceeded from Rearden's limited knowledge and desperate desire to protect his allegiance to his mills. Finally, Francisco secretly accepted Rearden's offer of a job as a furnace foreman so he could be there on the day when Rearden needed him in his final battle to liberate himself from the looters' clutches.

Rearden knows now that he is right to love and trust this man the way he always instinctively has. In their relationship, Ayn Rand dramatizes the meaning of friendship between rational men. The relationship is based exclusively on values, not on duty or self-sacrifice. Francisco and Rearden both revere productivity and the mind's ability to create prosperity on earth. Consequently, they deeply admire each other's accomplishments. Rand insists that, if human beings dedicate themselves to achievement rather than to selfless service, all humans can have this type of relationship. Francisco and Rearden, both of whom have lost Dagny, have found each other.

Part Three
Chapter 7—"This is John Galt Speaking"

Summary

The nation panics when Rearden retires. Under the looters' control, the newspapers print contradictory stories. Some papers say that he has quit, some that he was tragically killed in a car accident, and some that he is still working at his mills. But with Rearden gone, the output of the American steel industry drops precipitously. People despair for the future. Gangs of raiders terrorize the countryside, and acts of random violence proliferate. In response, the looters announce repeatedly that Mr. Thompson will speak to the country regarding the current crisis by radio broadcast on November 22. But at the appointed time, the Head of State is preempted. John Galt goes on the air instead and addresses the world. He tells the American people about the strike he has organized, including the reasons for it.

Commentary

The moment is right for John Galt to address the American people. With the imminent collapse of the American economy, his strike has served its purpose. The truth is now visible to everyone: The men of the mind create abundance. In their absence, all prosperity vanishes from the earth.

Galt explains the reasons for the strike—what he and the strikers stand for, and what they fight against. Galt presents the tenets of a revolutionary philosophy. He believes that reason is the only means by which human beings gain knowledge and create prosperity. He rejects faith and emotion as tools of cognition. He maintains that the universe is intelligible—that its fundamental principles are eternal, lawful, and immutable. He rejects the belief that the universe is created by and/or subject to the commands of any being, including a god, society, or some individual. Galt also argues that human beings must be rational in order to prosper or even survive on earth—and that they must *choose* to be rational. Man isn't a thinker automatically, nor is he sinful by nature, nor is he necessarily a whim-driven creature dominated by irrational desires. Man chooses between rationality and irrationality, between good and evil.

Galt believes that people must pursue their own self-interest—that the requirements of a person's existence necessitate that he seek his own values. Galt opposes any form of self-sacrifice or the renunciation of one's values. In Galt's philosophy, living by sacrificing one's values is impossible; life requires attaining those values. The code of self-sacrifice—whether the sacrifice is to God, society, or something else—is the code of death. Men who try to live by self-sacrifice end up destroying themselves.

Galt states that man needs political freedom to apply his intellect to pursuing the values that his life requires. He defends laissez-faire capitalism as the only political/economic system that recognizes man's need for liberty and the only system that protects his right to use his mind independently. Galt is opposed to socialism, fascism, communism, or any other type of system that tyrannizes the mind of man. The essence of his philosophy is that the mind is the source of human well-being, and the mind must be free.

Part Three
Chapter 8—The Egoist

Summary

After Galt's speech, the American people show signs of discontent with the looters' regime. Mr. Thompson wants to negotiate a deal with Galt. The looters broadcast repeated messages trying to reach Galt, but he doesn't reply. Thompson tells Dagny that he is worried. The pro-terror faction led by Floyd Ferris doesn't want to negotiate with Galt. That faction wants Galt dead, and Thompson isn't sure that he can prevent the murder. Thompson isn't even certain that Galt is still alive.

Terrified for Galt's safety, Dagny goes to his apartment. The looters follow her. Understanding what will happen as a result of her visit, Galt tells Dagny that she must pretend he is her enemy; otherwise, the looters will torture her to force his surrender. The looters arrest Galt and try to convince him to become the economic dictator of the country, but their pleas have no effect.

The American people don't believe that Galt will collaborate with the looters. Many don't even believe that he is in custody. As more people begin to starve, riots, open civil war in California, and the breakdown of civil authority ensue. One of the warring California factions has seized control of the rail station in San Francisco, so Taggart Transcontinental has no cross-country service. Eddie Willers flies to the West Coast to try to restore it. The looters announce the unveiling of the "John Galt Plan" to save the country's economy. However, when they try to televise their announcement to the country, Galt leans abruptly sideways to expose to the television cameras the gun being held to his ribs. "Get the hell out of my way," says Galt.

Commentary

Character Insight

Mr. Thompson's willingness to deal with Galt and his belief that a deal is possible are revealing. Thompson is an unprincipled pragmatist. He believes that ideas, theories, and principles have no role in human life. Action is all that matters. It doesn't matter to Thompson that Galt holds ideas regarding the nature of man, rights, society, and government that diametrically oppose the ideas embodied in the looters' system. Thompson believes that the looters will make some concessions to economic freedom, Galt will accept the chance to run the economy, and both sides will strike a deal. Galt will then figure out some way to make the mongrel system of clashing principles work.

Ferris and his faction, which advocates terror, show much greater philosophical understanding than Mr. Thompson. Because the looters, including Mr. Thompson, have no intention of relinquishing power, no possibility of compromise with an advocate of individual rights and political freedom exists. Galt is their deadliest foe. If he succeeds, a place doesn't exist for the looters or their power-lusting policies in the free society to come. Galt, therefore, must be killed. The pro-terror faction is right—there is no middle ground between freedom and dictatorship. Individuals either have rights or they are slaves. Looters either maintain their dictatorship, or Galt's ideas lead to freedom. A compromise between these contradictory alternatives isn't possible.

Theme

The events in this chapter make clear one of Ayn Rand's ongoing themes: Humans face a fundamental choice between the intellect and brute force. The men of reason, like Galt and the strikers, understand that the mind functions independently. A human being can only survive by means of his mind, so he must be free to act on his own best judgment. Political freedom is a logical necessity for survival. The men who reject reason, like the looters, have no means to survive. They can't cure diseases, invent airplanes, run a transcontinental railroad, or build the John Galt Line. Conquering the men of the mind is the only way the irrational brutes can survive. The naked tyranny of dictatorship is the logical outcome of rejecting the mind as man's means of survival. Men live by reason, or they attempt to live by force. There is no third alternative. Hence, Rand paints the sad spectacle of the brutes seeking to force the mind to become economic dictator.

Glossary

egoist a person who believes in the doctrine that self-interest is the proper goal of all human actions. Here, it refers to Galt's recognition that his self-interest lies in refusing to surrender his mind to the demands of the looters.

Part Three
Chapter 9—The Generator

Summary

Robert Stadler realizes that regardless of the outcome of events in Washington, he has no place there. If Galt wins, Stadler will be rejected as a traitor to the mind's cause. But if the looters win, he'll be subordinate to a pack of ignorant dolts whom he despises. In the chaos of increasing civil war, Stadler needs to carve out a kingdom of his own. He drives to the Project X site in Iowa, intending to employ the deadly weapon as a means to establish his own fiefdom, but Cuffy Meigs beat him to it. In the ensuing power struggle, the weapon is activated, cutting a swath of destruction for hundreds of square miles, killing everybody at the installation, including Stadler.

The looters take Galt to the State Science Institute, where they use torture in an attempt to force him to fold. Dagny calls Francisco, who left her a number for such a contingency. While she prepares to go in search of Galt, a railroad engineer contacts her, letting her know that the vital Taggart Bridge spanning the Mississippi was destroyed by the Project X explosion. Dagny says that she doesn't know what to do about that problem, and she leaves to join Francisco.

At the State Science Institute, the looters torture Galt. When the torture device breaks down, the looters don't know how to repair it. Galt instructs them how to fix the device. James Taggart, in the act of trying to break Galt, realizes that his life is dedicated to the destruction of the good, and in that moment he recognizes his own unmitigated evil. He collapses, unable to live with such knowledge.

Commentary

Robert Stadler, the genius turned feudal baron, dramatizes the principle that men seek to live by either mind or force. Holding an elitist belief that only a select few are interested in ideas and that most men are irrational brutes, Stadler necessarily believes that reason is impotent in dealing with people and that only intimidation and force are effective weapons. He is then driven by the logic of his theory to become a looter, a power seeker, and ultimately, Galt's worst enemy. The form of his death is not ironic; his death is the exact end dictated by the logic of his life. He placed his mind in service to the brutes and is killed by the weapon that his research created for them.

Galt, knowing the logical inevitability of Stadler's end, refuses to turn his mind over to the purveyors of force. He uses his mind only to create and defend the values necessary for life on earth. Even the help that he gives the looters to repair the instrument of torture is an action taken in defense of himself and against the looters, because he shows them that they're dependent on him even for the most evil purposes. The irrational live off the men of the mind, and Galt drives this point home to them. Galt, the preeminent man of the mind, is the generator of progress and prosperity.

Dagny, knowing that the looters are willing to torture and kill Galt, finally understands their true nature. Previously, Dagny believed that the looters had a will to live, but were mistaken about how to do so. Now she realizes that in forsaking the mind in favor of brute force, they've given up on human life. They support a code of death: Destruction is all that their policies can lead to, and destruction is their goal. Their willingness to torture Galt is significant because Galt represents the mind. No man who would torture the mind can claim life as his goal. Dagny sees the irredeemable evil of the looters and the necessity to withdraw her mind from their system. Dagny joins the strike with the act of walking away from the Taggart Bridge disaster.

Part Three
Chapter 10—In the Name of the Best Within Us

Summary

Rearden, Dagny, Ragnar, and Francisco rescue Galt from his tor-
turers, and they fly back to the valley. Eddie Willers, after days of nego-
tiation, has reopened the Taggart station in San Francisco and restored
transcontinental service. He rides the Comet, attempting to return to
New York, but it breaks down in Arizona, and he and the crew are
unable to repair the engine. The crew and passengers desert the stranded
Comet for a passing covered wagon. Eddie refuses to leave the train.
He'll get it moving or will die attempting to do so.

The looters' regime finally collapses, and Galt gives word that the
strikers will now return and rebuild the world.

Commentary

The torture of John Galt is the looters' last futile effort to save their
system. They refuse to understand, though the evidence is all around
them, that the mind requires freedom to think and create. They cling
to their belief that force is the most effective method for dealing with
people. Galt refuses to become economic czar because he recognizes
that such a plan is hopeless. Economic production can be restored only
when the innovative minds are free to act on their own: to invent and
create new products, start their own companies, manufacture the goods,
and make money by selling to customers on an open market. The looters, refusing to lift the stifling controls on the mind, have no chance to
restore economic prosperity.

Theme

The fundamental conflict in this story is the mind versus brute
force. The final resolution of the conflict holds true to its essence:
Despite the looters' attempts to enslave the mind through force, Galt
emerges victorious in his commitment to his intellectual freedom. The
mind is the power that moves the world. Any force working against
the mind must, ultimately, collapse from its own ineptitude.

The looters' system overcomes Eddie Willers before its final collapse. Train service, like all the other accomplishments of a technologically advanced society, is disintegrating. Society is reverting to covered wagons and candles. Eddie, committed to the mind and its achievements, refuses to abandon the train, but Eddie doesn't understand enough engineering to repair the locomotive. He doesn't share the intellectual abilities of Dagny, Rearden, or Galt. Therefore, his fate depends on the strikers. Will Dagny and Francisco find their friend in the vast desert? Or will Eddie perish in the wilderness? Clearly, he deserves to be in the valley, but will the valley's residents succeed in rescuing him? Rand deliberately leaves Eddie's situation unresolved. She shows that the fate of Eddie Willers—who represents every man at his *moral* best—is dependent on the fate of the great minds. When the geniuses are free to think and create, the common man flourishes. But when the great thinkers are stifled, the common man suffers. Dagny can only do her best in attempting to find her loyal friend amidst the violent chaos that the looters' system has generated.

CHARACTER ANALYSES

The following character analyses delve into the physical, emotional, and psychological traits of the literary work's major characters so that you might better understand what motivates these characters. The writer of this study guide provides this scholarship as an educational tool by which you may compare your own interpretations of the characters. Before reading the character analyses that follow, consider first writing your own short essays on the characters as an exercise by which you can test your understanding of the original literary work. Then, compare your essays to those that follow, noting discrepancies between the two. If your essays appear lacking, that might indicate that you need to re-read the original literary work or re-familiarize yourself with the major characters.

John Galt

Galt is the hero and main character of *Atlas Shrugged,* because his principles drive the action and the conflict of the story. The book explores what occurs when the thinkers go on strike. Galt conceives of the strike, initiates it, sustains it, and carries it to a successful resolution. Part of the fascination of *Atlas Shrugged* is that its dominant character works behind the scenes, his existence unknown to the reader, for the first two-thirds of the novel. The question invoking his name lends a legendary quality to his character, as if he were, in part, a mythological being. In a universe populated with giants, his is the character of greatest stature. The mystery shrouding the story's unfolding conflict results from the choices he makes. The strike is necessarily secretive, so the disappearance of the world's great thinkers must be a mystery to everyone outside of Galt's circle.

Galt realizes, during the implementation of communist principles at the Twentieth Century Motor Company, that the only hope of ending the mind's exploitation is by means of a strike. His insight has the potential to usher in a new historical period—to be "epoch-making."

Ayn Rand presents Galt as a man of epic proportions. She stated that the goal of her writing was the presentation of an ideal man, and that goal is reached with the figure of John Galt. He is a man of prodigious intellectual gifts—a physicist who brings about a revolution in man's understanding of energy, a philosopher who defines a rational view of existence, and a statesman who leads a strike that transfigures the social systems of the world. Two characteristics make possible the enormity of his intellectual achievements. One is his unique genius. The other is a trait that men can replicate: his unswerving rationality. Galt describes himself as "the man who loves his life," which is accurate. But above all, he is the man who perceives reality—the man who allows nothing to interfere with his cognitive apprehension of the facts. He is characterized by reference to his "ruthlessly perceptive eyes"—the eyes that honor facts and see reality for what it is, regardless of Galt's feelings about that reality.

In a signature scene, Galt tells Dagny—the woman he has loved and watched for years—what he did and felt upon learning that she was Hank Rearden's mistress. He went to observe Rearden at an industrialists' conference. Rearden had everything that Galt wanted and could have had if he hadn't chosen to strike. Rearden had his mills, his invention, his wealth, his fame, and his love relationship with Dagny. For one moment, Galt felt a tearing sense of loss. He saw what would have been his if he hadn't abandoned his motor. But Galt felt that loss for only a moment, because he then recognized the full set of facts defining the situation. He saw the burdens that Rearden carried, the impossible demands, and the forces stifling and enslaving him. He saw Rearden struggling in silent agony, striving to understand what Galt alone had understood. He saw Rearden for what he was—the symbol of the strike, the great unrewarded hero whom Galt was to liberate and validate. The scene that he describes to Dagny provides the key to understanding Galt's character. He feels intense emotion and suffers when he experiences loss, but he doesn't permit his emotions to interfere with his cognitive grasp of reality or with his actions based on that cognition. He knows that the strike is right, and no pain resulting from its consequences can defile the purity of his cognition.

What makes Galt unique is his method of using his mind—his unflinching commitment to facts, even if they are unpleasant, painful, or frightening. He functions rationally, holding an undeviating allegiance to reality that his most honest judgment grasps. Galt's life embodies a proactive eagerness to seek out truth and an inviolable willingness to accept it, no matter its content. He recognizes that man can only achieve success and happiness by revering reality. He doesn't consider facing reality a duty or something that requires tight-lipped stoicism. Instead, he celebrates reality, joyously recognizing that consistent adherence to reality is at the core of self-interest. He knows that a willful departure from reality is the essence of self-destruction.

John Galt is a hero representing the best of modern civilization—its science, its medical research, its technological progress, and its application of intellect in service to human life. He embodies the novel's essential theme: Only by means of the mind can human beings achieve prosperity on earth.

Because of the towering achievements of his intellect, it's easy to overlook the other aspects of Galt's life: his light, effortless way of moving; his passionate love for Dagny; the tenderness and concern he shows for his lifelong friends, Francisco d'Anconia and Ragnar Danneskjöld; and his respect for his teacher/spiritual father, Hugh Akston. The special bond that Galt shares with these four people shows Rand's rejection of the conventional split between reason and emotion, which holds that an individual can be either rational or emotional—he cannot be both. The poignant, understated intensity of Galt's relief on seeing Ragnar after a year of ceaseless dangers is a simple but eloquent example of a rational man's emotional life. Because Galt values the mind and its achievements, he must give his love to exalted individuals. A man of reason cannot look unmoved upon such noble souls as Francisco, Ragnar, and Dagny. A true man of the mind experiences the most intense emotional bond to such individuals *because* he is a man of the mind. In the character of John Galt, Ayn Rand shows that reason and emotion can and should be integrated in the human being's life.

Dagny Taggart

Dagny is the heroine and primary narrator of the story. Her great stature comes from the combination of characteristics that she possesses. Her knowledge of engineering and industry enables her to expertly run a transcontinental railroad. Her understanding of physics allows her to identify the virtues of Rearden Metal. The independence of her judgment lets her stand by the metal and her railroad in the face of virtually unanimous social opposition. Her dauntless determination drives her to build the John Galt Line. The qualities that make Dagny a towering character are the same qualities that make real-life individuals such as the scientist Marie Curie and the innovative educator Maria Montessori great heroines. Like these women, Dagny has an unswerving dedication to truth, regardless of social opinion. The dedication to truth supports her ability to discover new knowledge and create new products.

The same attributes that make Dagny great also make John Galt great—and Aristotle, Michangelo, Leonardo da Vinci, and Isaac Newton. Rand dramatizes a crucial point in Dagny's character: Human greatness equals rational achievement irrespective of gender. Great human beings employ their intellectual ability to create the values on which human life depends. Stature of character is not gender-specific.

A reader may question why Rand portrays Dagny as an engineer—as a genius specifically in the field of heavy industry. If Rand's purpose is to portray a woman's intellectual prowess—to show that a gender-based difference between a woman's cognitive functioning and a man's doesn't exist—why not present her as a great writer, mathematician, theoretical scientist, composer, or artist? Why does she portray her as a brilliantly creative industrialist? In addition to the relevant plot considerations, Dagny's career path makes a philosophical point: If intellect is more life-giving than brawn, then women can run machinery, create new physical products, invent, innovate, oversee heavy industry, raise the material standard of living, and so on. The human intellect, regardless of gender, shapes the physical environment in order to meet human survival requirements. Ayn Rand doesn't believe that faith can move mountains. However, in the character of Dagny Taggart, Rand shows that a rational woman can create and deploy the technology to move mountains just as effectively as a rational man.

Like Galt, Dagny is much more than a pure intellect. Her emotional life is equally as intense as Galt's, and for the same reason. The men of the mind value man's life on earth; they love the industry, technology, and science that promote life. They feel enormous admiration and attraction for the giants among mankind who are responsible for progress. This admiration and attraction is why Dagny falls to her hands and knees, dirty and disheveled, shaking with excitement and screaming for Rearden, when she realizes the nature of the abandoned scrap of a motor she finds in a junk pile. This same admiration and attraction is why her body aches with a desire for Galt that verges on physical pain when she is in his home in the valley, and is why she races desperately back to New York when she hears the news of the Taggart Tunnel disaster. Dagny has committed mind, body, and soul to man's life on earth—and to the achievements and achievers that make life on earth possible.

Hank Rearden

Ayn Rand's philosophy of Objectivism stresses the virtue of productivity—the ability of human beings to create the goods and services necessary for survival on earth. Hank Rearden is the embodiment of this virtue. In his early teens, Rearden pushed himself to herculean efforts in the ore mines, refusing to acknowledge pain and exhaustion as legitimate grounds to stop working. Later, he bought the mines and worked virtually 20-hour days to build a vast, steel-producing empire. Through 10 years of prodigious effort, he created a new metal alloy far superior to steel. His productivity is legendary, even among the other industrial giants in the valley. Andrew Stockton, owner of the country's best foundry, says that Rearden would put him out of business if he ever joined the strike and entered the valley: "'But boy! I'd work for him as a cinder sweeper. He'd blast through this valley like a rocket. He'd triple everybody's production.'"

Productivity is the adaptation of nature to man's survival needs. It involves the creation of goods and services that human life requires.

Because nothing is given to man on earth—and all must be created—productivity is a major moral virtue. The mind is the source of all wealth, the means by which man creates economic value and reshapes the physical environment. Consequently, productivity is an expression of the principle of mind-body integration, the ability of the mind to create material abundance for the purpose of enjoying life on earth. But Hank Rearden holds, through much of the story, a mistaken premise that prevents him from recognizing his own moral greatness. He believes the theory that mind and body are split. This viewpoint is known as the mind-body dichotomy—the belief that the mind or soul belongs to a "higher" world superior to this one, and that earth is ruled by the "low" instincts of the body. Rearden's liberation from this way of thinking transforms his character.

Because Rearden initially regards the body as base or ignoble, he devalues all of its activities. He initially berates both Dagny and himself for their passionate lovemaking. He also says to her, in the context of discussing the unlimited potential of Rearden Metal, "We're a couple of blackguards, aren't we? We haven't any spiritual goals or qualities. All we're after is material things. That's all we care for." Early in the story, he isn't able to recognize the great virtue that his productivity or his relationship with Dagny represents.

Rearden's friendship with Francisco teaches him that material production is an intellectual process and a sublime virtue. His relationship with Dagny teaches him that sex involves the expression of an individual's deepest beliefs and values; he is attracted to her because she represents the same values of rationality and industrial productivity that he cherishes. Only when Rearden throws off the idea that the body and its concerns are low is he able to recognize his own superlative value.

Francisco d'Anconia

Francisco is one of John Galt's two closest friends and an indispensable ally in the strike. He takes on the role of squandering playboy as cover for his two real activities. One of these is to gradually obliterate all assets of the world's wealthiest corporation—d'Anconia Copper—and in so doing, to help destroy other industrial concerns, such as Taggart Transcontinental. His other purpose is to recruit great thinkers for the strike. More than anyone else, Francisco helps liberate Hank Rearden from the shackles of the self-sacrifice ethics, enabling Rearden to recognize the virtue and necessity of the strike.

The swashbuckling gaiety and enthusiasm that define Francisco's character result from his view of the world—a view that Ayn Rand terms the *benevolent universe premise*. This theory holds that reality is open to the achievements of rational men. Human beings who recognize that rational thought and productive effort alone advance their lives, and who don't place their whims above facts, can expect to attain their goals and live in happiness. Francisco's recognition of this truth is expressed in the two refrains of his childhood. "Let's find out!" was his way to motivate Dagny and Eddie to embark on a new adventure. "Let's make it" was his call to engage in acts of construction. The first expresses an explorer's premise, the second a builder's. Both represent a man to whom reality is open, an individual for whom all roads are cleared and green lights stretch to the horizon.

Even Francisco's characteristic mockery, his use of irony and biting derision, is always benevolent and positive. He always directs his mockery at the irrational, never at the good and never at strangers. He laughs openly at people like James Taggart, because he knows that man can and should be much better. While James Taggart uses derision as a weapon of destruction, Francisco uses it as a means of destroying the destroyers, thereby clearing the road for the creative. His trademark mockery always supports his values. A scene from his childhood proves this point. When a professor of literature saw Francisco on top of a pile in a junk yard, happily "dismantling the carcass of an automobile," he said, "'A young man of your position ought to spend his time in libraries, absorbing the culture of the world.'" Francisco replied, "'What do you think I'm doing?'" He didn't intend to needle or insult the professor. He intended to expand the meaning of the term "culture" to recognize the profound value of technology and industrial production. Even at such a young age, Francisco focused on making a positive point.

Francisco's life-giving benevolence is shown in his love for Hank Rearden. The injustice of Rearden being enslaved and exploited by his family and the looting politicians is deeply moving to Francisco. He undertakes the long process of teaching Rearden to check his moral premises—to reject both the mind-body dichotomy and the self-sacrifice ethic. He receives both insults and a physical blow from Rearden but brushes them aside. He tells Rearden that if he saw Atlas straining with his last ounce of strength to support the world for a final instant before he expired, he would tell him to shrug, to release the self-sacrificial responsibility, and to recognize his own right to live.

Francisco does more than save Rearden's life during the assault on the mills; he shows him the reality of a new life. Francisco's unceasing campaign bears fruit when Rearden understands the senseless futility of cannibalizing the productive and virtuous for the sake of vicious moochers. Francisco's work is complete when Rearden throws off the shackles of guilt and servitude binding him to the parasites and joyously recognizes his own inestimable moral value. Francisco, recruiting agent for the strike, wins his greatest conquest.

James Taggart

Taggart is the president of Taggart Transcontinental, Dagny's older brother, and the novel's most prominent villain. He is far worse than a corrupt businessman seeking wealth by parasitical means. Like his soulmate Lillian Rearden, Taggart is riddled with hatred for the good. His goal in life, which dominates his actions even when he doesn't recognize it explicitly, is to disfigure and destroy the men of the mind. He is a *nihilist*, one who seeks destruction of the good, and this characteristic dominates all aspects of his life.

Nihilism explains why Taggart hates Francisco, Dagny, Rearden, and Wyatt. It explains why he wants to hear Galt scream. It's also his primary motive for cannibalizing the Phoenix-Durango Railroad and destroying Dan Conway. To wound Hank Rearden is Taggart's sole reason for having sex with Lillian. To destroy the innocent hero-worship of Cherryl Brooks is his sole reason for marrying her. Taggart wants to celebrate the announcement of Argentina's transformation into a "People's State" not because of his anticipated profit, but because of the nationalization of d'Anconia Copper and the resulting financial destruction of Francisco d'Anconia.

Because man cannot live with the conscious realization that his purpose in life is destruction, Taggart is forced to evade understanding his true motives. He lies to himself endlessly, trying to convince himself that he seeks to gain wealth, to protect the interests of his railroad, to help "friends" such as Orren Boyle, or to serve the "public welfare." The truth is that Taggart doesn't value wealth, life, the railroad, success, Boyle, or the public. If "value" means to have a strong positive commitment to some life-enhancing person, object, or process, Taggart values nothing. On the contrary, he hates people capable of achieving values and living successfully. He is riddled with envy, which Ayn Rand defines as "hatred of the good for being the good." Only one thing compels him: to wreak such devastation that the good have no chance to survive. This is why, during a meeting that leads to the passage of Directive 10-289 (the laws designed to enslave productive men), Taggart involuntarily screams, "If we are to perish, let's make sure that we all perish together. Let's make sure that we leave them no chance to survive!"

Taggart's wanton destruction of Cherryl leaves him shaken because it brings his true motivation too near to the surface; the fabric of lies designed to protect him from the truth is in danger of crumbling under the strain. When he has Galt—the ultimate example of man's capacity to live and the symbol of all that he hates—in his power, his kill-lust peaks. He doesn't merely want to hear Galt scream; he wants Galt to die. When that realization bursts through into his explicit awareness, the motivation for his entire existence stands naked before him. No man can withstand the recognition of his own utter moral depravity. Taggart has evaded this recognition his entire life, and realizing this dreaded knowledge causes him to lose his mind.

Taggart endorses the doctrines of altruism and collectivism because they enable him to attack and enslave the productive men that he hates. He recognizes that the consistent application of these theories leads inevitably to national socialism and communism, which are totalitarian dictatorships that imprison and exterminate the independent minds that he loathes. The acts of mass destruction wreaked by such collectivist murderers as Adolf Hitler, Joseph Stalin, Mao Tse-tung, and Pol Pot are chilling real-life examples of the same nihilism that drives the actions of James Taggart. In Taggart's character, Ayn Rand lays bare the underlying premises of mankind's most evil representatives.

CRITICAL ESSAYS

On the pages that follow, the writer of this study guide provides critical scholarship on various aspects of Rand's *Atlas Shrugged*. These interpretive essays are intended solely to enhance your understanding of the original literary work; they are supplemental materials and are not to replace your reading of *Atlas Shrugged*. When you're finished reading *Atlas Shrugged*, and prior to your reading this study guide's critical essays, consider making a bulleted list of what you think are the most important themes and symbols. Write a short paragraph under each bullet explaining why you think that theme or symbol is important; include at least one short quote from the original literary work that supports your contention. Then, test your list and reasons against those found in the following essays. Do you include themes and symbols that the study guide author doesn't? If so, this self test might indicate that you are well on your way to understanding original literary work. But if not, perhaps you will need to re-read *Atlas Shrugged*.

The Role of the Mind in Human Life

All the main positive characters in *Atlas Shrugged* are great minds. Dagny Taggart is a brilliant businesswoman/engineer who runs a transcontinental railroad superbly. Hank Rearden is a productive genius of the steel industry and an extraordinary metallurgist who invents a new material that's vastly superior to steel. Francisco d'Anconia is a prodigy who masters every task as quickly as it's presented to him, independently develops a crude version of differential equations at age 12, and invents a new kind of copper smelter. Ellis Wyatt is an innovator of the oil industry who creates an advanced method of extracting oil from shale rock. Ragnar Danneskjöld is a brilliant philosopher, and Hugh Akston, his teacher, is the last great advocate of reason. Above all towers John Galt, a philosopher, scientist, inventor, statesman, and man of superlative genius and accomplishment who, in real life, can be compared only to the greatest minds of human history. The heroes in *Atlas Shrugged* all dramatize the novel's theme: The mind is mankind's tool of survival.

In *Atlas Shrugged,* every advance that makes human life on earth possible is a product of the reasoning mind. The creation of the John Galt Line requires Dagny's engineering knowledge, the creation of Rearden Metal requires Rearden's understanding of metallurgy, and the invention of Galt's motor requires his command of physics. All inventions, breakthroughs, and innovations are creations of the mind, including the production of items that human beings require for day-to-day survival. *Atlas Shrugged* reminds us that the ability to successfully grow food involves knowledge of agricultural science; building houses relies on comprehension of architecture, engineering, and mathematics; and curing diseases requires knowledge of medicine. If man is to resolve various forms of mental illness, he must know psychology. If he is to establish a free society, he must understand the principles of political philosophy. If man is to avert war, or even personal conflict, he must be able to negotiate his differences, which requires reason. Every value that human life depends on is a product of the reasoning mind. This idea is Ayn Rand's thesis in *Atlas Shrugged.*

The villains in *Atlas Shrugged* avoid rationality and production, seeking survival instead by looting the producers. The villains attempt to live by brute force, not by reason. However, man is not a tiger or a shark; he can't survive the same way animals do. Animals survive by devouring each other, and nature equips them to battle for survival by exclusively physical means. Each species possesses its survival instrument. Birds have wings, lions have claws and fangs, antelopes enjoy speed, elephants utilize size, gorillas showcase their strength, and so on, but man can't survive by these means. He lacks wings, claws, great size, strength, or speed. Nature endows man with but one instrument by means of which to survive—his mind.

Dagny, Rearden, Galt, and the other thinkers live in accordance with their rational nature. Wesley Mouch, James Taggart, Floyd Ferris, and the other villains in the story seek survival by means of force, which is an animal's method, not a man's. Consequently, the villains have no more chance to succeed than a bird that refuses to use its wings. The looters can—and, at times in real life, do—destroy the creators. But having abandoned their survival instrument, they lack all chance of achieving flourishing, joyous lives. Once they ruin the producers, they are left to starve. Only the men of the mind can attain prosperity.

In order to fully understand Ayn Rand's theme in *Atlas Shrugged,* we must contrast it with its opposites. Objectivism's claim that the mind is the fundamental means by which man survives contrasts with the claims of the two dominant philosophical schools of modern western culture, Marxism and Christianity. The Marxists maintain that manual labor is the means by which human beings produce economic value: Muscle power, not brain power, creates wealth. Marxists believe that the physical workers create economic commodities and the capitalists exploit the workers. Ben Nealy, the contractor with whom Dagny is stuck after McNamara's retirement, expresses Marx's belief succinctly when he claims, "Muscles, Miss Taggart, that's all it takes to build anything in the world." Ayn Rand's answer to Marx is contained on every page of *Atlas Shrugged.* How much manual labor (muscle power) does it take to create Galt's motor, Rearden's Metal, or Wyatt's innovative process of extracting oil from shale? In real life, how much muscle power was required to invent Edison's light bulb, design Frank Lloyd Wright's buildings, discover methods for heart transplant surgery, or create Fulton's steamboat? Obviously, no amount of muscle power is sufficient to create these products on its own, because they first require breakthroughs in knowledge. The mind is fundamentally responsible for these innovations and countless others. Manual labor is part of constructing new products after they're designed, but the brain performs the original act of design, not the biceps.

Christianity's view is that man survives by faith in God—that strong, pure faith can move mountains. But Ayn Rand argues that all the faith in the world is inadequate to move one grain of sand one millimeter. If human beings seek to move mountains in order to construct interstate highway systems or transcontinental railroads, they can do so only by means of dynamite, technology, and science. Faith in God cannot enable Dagny and Rearden (or their real-life equivalents) to build railroad lines, invent metals, or design new bridges. Only rigorous thought can reach such accomplishments. The mind—not faith in the supernatural— grows food and cures diseases. Likewise, only societies that are scientifically, technologically, and industrially advanced—such as the modern United States—have high living standards. Places and eras dominated by faith, such as Europe during the Middle and Dark Ages, are backward and destitute. When the mind is absent—whether on strike, as in the novel, or subordinated to faith, as in Medieval Europe—the result is regression into a cultural dark age.

Great creative minds such as Galt's, by definition, think new thoughts and discover new knowledge. They neither conform to social belief nor obey a tyrant's command. They follow their own vision and pursue their own truth. In making intellectual breakthroughs, people like John Galt lead mankind's progress. This idea, too, is part of Ayn Rand's theme in *Atlas Shrugged*: The mind must be free. Galt's strike is a declaration of independence for the intellectual. The strike shows that the mind can't and won't function under compulsion. Freedom is required for Rearden to create his metal, for Galt to invent his motor, or for any innovator to discover new truths. The creative mind looks only at the facts, whether of metallurgy, energy conversion, or another field. It does not bow to the whims of a dictator. If people like Floyd Ferris or Wesley Mouch can, by decree, stifle or redirect the research being done by a Galt or a Rearden, they've placed a gun between the great mind and the facts that it studies. This explains why the freest countries are the most advanced, and why the brutal dictatorships that proliferate across the globe wallow in backwardness and abysmal poverty. Galt's strike recognizes that the first right of human beings is the freedom to think and act independently. The result of this freedom is the unshackling of the human mind and a dramatic rise in living standards.

The Role of the Common Man in *Atlas Shrugged:* The Eddie Willers Story

The heroes of *Atlas Shrugged* are men and women of great intellect. Dagny, Rearden, Francisco, Ellis Wyatt, and, above all, Galt are superb thinkers—even geniuses. The story makes clear the multitude of ways in which the great minds are mankind's benefactors. But an honest reader may ask: What about the common man? Do heroism and moral stature require extraordinary intellectual ability, or can individuals of more modest intelligence aspire to these lofty goals? What is the relationship between a man's intelligence and his moral character? In *Atlas Shrugged*, Ayn Rand gives her answer to these questions through the character of Eddie Willers.

Eddie lacks the genius possessed by his boss, Dagny Taggart. He is her diligent, able assistant, but he's not capable of building the John Galt Line, judging the merit of Rearden Metal, identifying the nature of the abandoned motor, finding a scientist capable of reconstructing the motor, or resolving the chaos that the Taggart Tunnel explosion causes. Likewise, he doesn't possess the ability to run Taggart Transcontinental. He even states, in his forthright manner, that he isn't a great man. He knows that if the railroad goes, he won't be able to rebuild it; if such a tragedy occurs, he'll share its demise.

But the issue of Eddie's character is of greater importance. He is as constant in his devotion to the railroad as Dagny. He works the same long hours willingly; he stands at her side through every crisis; he is equally shocked and outraged at the behavior of James Taggart and the looters. Eddie has known, from early childhood, that the railroad is his life. In response to James Taggart's snide reference to him becoming a feudal serf tied to Taggart Transcontinental, Eddie states, "That's what I am."

Like Dagny, Eddie reveres the achievements of Ellis Wyatt, Hank Rearden, and the unknown inventor of the motor. Eddie is, in the words Rand uses to describe Dagny, a child of the Industrial Revolution. He recognizes the benefits to human life from inventions like Rearden Metal and Galt's motor, from new methods like Ellis Wyatt's process for extracting oil from shale, and from industrial production, like that attained by Rearden Steel. In his lifelong devotion to the railroad, Eddie demonstrates his commitment to industry and technology, to the scientific research necessary to create them, and to the mind's role in promoting human wellness on earth. The theme of *Atlas Shrugged* is the life-giving nature of rationality, and Eddie is as dedicated to the mind as any of the great thinkers in the story.

Eddie doesn't possess the brainpower of Dagny, Rearden, or Galt, but he is as fully rational as they are. Galt explains that rationality is a commitment to the facts—an inviolable willingness to face reality, no matter how painful, frightening, or unpleasant the truth may be in a specific case. Rationality means never placing any consideration above one's honest grasp of the facts. Eddie practices this method as fully as Galt. His rationality is shown throughout the story, but his early dialogue with James Taggart regarding the Rio Norte Line is a specific example. Eddie tells Taggart that there's been another wreck, the track is shot, and the Phoenix-Durango provides superior service. Eddie also says that the railroad can't wait any longer for Orren Boyle to deliver new rails. Taggart argues that if his company can't get the rail because of unavoidable delays at Associated Steel, nobody can blame him for Taggart Transcontinental's shoddy track or poor service. Eddie seeks to fix the track, but James Taggart only looks to avoid blame. Where Eddie is concerned with the facts, Taggart's sole regard is for public opinion. The difference between their specific concerns reflects the deeper difference between their cognitive methods. Taggart's thinking is ruled by the opinions of others; facts rule Eddie's thoughts.

Eddie's character demonstrates the difference between intelligence and rationality. Intelligence is intellectual *ability*, whereas rationality is a *method*. Intelligence is a capacity for understanding, but rationality is a means of using one's mind. Robert Stadler, for example, has incomparably greater intelligence than Eddie, but Eddie is far more rational. Stadler has the genius to make significant advances in theoretical physics, but when dealing with men, he often evades or denies important facts. Stadler tries to convince himself that Galt is dead—"he has to be," he says—and that no connection exists between the prodigy he taught at Patrick Henry University and the man of whom the entire world speaks. Most important, Stadler tries to deny the truth of John Galt's words, though he knows that all of Galt's words are true. He repeatedly pushes aside the realization that, in aligning himself with the brutes, he has betrayed the mind. Unlike Stadler, Eddie refuses to push facts aside no matter how painful or frightening they are. He doesn't deny that the economy is collapsing; that, when the railroad goes, he'll go with it; or that Dagny, the woman he loves, is sleeping with Rearden. Eddie faces reality at all times. He merely possesses limited intellectual ability with which to do so.

Atlas Shrugged shows that intellect is necessary to promote man's prosperity on earth. The achievements of Rearden, Dagny, Galt, and the other thinkers dramatize the claim that reason is the primary cause of progress. But intellectual ability isn't within a man's volitional control. The ability of his brain is something that a man is born with, but he chooses whether he uses it. Eddie's consistent choice to accept the responsibility of thinking is the hallmark of a virtuous man. An individual can be judged only by what is subject to his control. On issues that are open to his choice, Eddie is a man of great stature.

Morality, according to the theme of *Atlas Shrugged*, involves an unbreached commitment to the rational requirements of man's life on earth. Eddie exhibits such commitment to the end. For example, when the Taggart Comet breaks down in the Arizona desert, the passengers and crew abandon it for a covered wagon, but Eddie refuses to leave the train. "We can't let it go!" Eddie says fiercely. At some level, he knows that he means more than the Comet and the railroad. Eddie won't abandon industrial production, technology, science, and progress; he refuses to revert to primitive modes of transport or living. He'll fix the train and restore transcontinental service, or he'll die trying. He is loyal to the achievements of modern civilization and the minds that make them possible. This loyalty is the essence of his moral stature.

Ayn Rand deliberately leaves Eddie's fate unresolved. His friends may rescue him and take him to the valley, where he deserves to be, but it's also possible that Dagny and Francisco will be unable to find him in the desert and he'll die. Eddie's dependence on the strikers is a final example of the relationship between the common man and the creative geniuses. When the great minds are free to act upon their thoughts, they create abundance and the common man flourishes. However, when geniuses are enslaved, they're unable to generate prosperity, and the common man suffers as a result. Eddie Willers—the moral best of every man—understands this truth. His moral status lies in his veneration of the mind.

CliffsNotes Review

Use this CliffsNotes Review to test your understanding of the original text and to reinforce what you've learned in this book. After you work through the quotation identifications, practice projects, and discussion questions, you're well on your way to understanding a comprehensive and meaningful interpretation of Rand's *Atlas Shrugged*.

Q&A

1. One of the leading strikers masquerading as a squandering playboy is:

  a. Eddie Willers

  b. Francisco d'Anconia

  c. Robert Stadler

  d. Ragnar Danneskjöld

2. The railroad industrialist who builds the John Galt Line is:

  a. James Taggart

  b. Hank Rearden

  c. Dagny Taggart

  d. Dan Conway

3. As a means of fighting the looters, Ragnar Danneskjöld becomes a:

  a. pirate

  b. philosopher

  c. playboy

  d. politician

4. John Galt abandons his motor because:

  a. He must do so to conduct the strike.

  b. Nobody wants it.

  c. It doesn't work.

  d. The looters forbid its use.

5. Dagny Taggart pursues John Galt because:

  a. He is the inventor of the motor.

  b. He is the "destroyer" who drains the brains of the world.

  c. He is the man she loves.

  d. All of the above.

6. John Galt makes a radio address to the country because:

  a. He intends to announce and explain the strike.

  b. He doesn't like listening to Mr. Thompson.

  c. He wants to sell his motor.

  d. He seeks to impress Dagny.

  Answers: (1) b. (2) c. (3) a. (4) a. (5) d. (6) a.

Fill in the Blank

1. The theme of *Atlas Shrugged* is _____.

2. Dagny Taggart refuses to join the strike because _____.

3. Lillian Rearden's purpose is to _____.

4. Ragnar Danneskjöld gives gold to Hank Rearden because _____.

5. James Taggart destroys Cherryl because _____.

6. The strikers move to a remote valley in the Colorado Rockies because _____.

  Answers: (1) the importance of the mind to man's existence. (2) she is unwilling to give up her railroad. (3) destroy her husband. (4) he wants to serve justice, restoring to Rearden part of the money stolen from him. (5) she is a hero worshipper, and he hates all heroes. (6) the looters' system will collapse as a result of the great minds' absence.

Identify the Quotation

1. What can you do when you have to deal with people?

2. Who is John Galt?

3. I'm the man who robs the poor and gives to the rich.

4. The sight of an achievement was the greatest gift a human being could offer to others.

5. Don't you understand that the Rio Norte Line is breaking up—whether anybody blames us or not?

6. Contradictions cannot exist. Whenever you think that you are facing a contradiction, check your premises. You will find that one of them is wrong.

Answers: (1) Robert Stadler says this on several occasions. He believes that most human beings are irrational and can be ruled only by force. (2) Many people ask this question. Some ask it ironically, but most pessimistically. The question is an expression of despair and hopelessness. (3) Ragnar Danneskjöld explains to Hank Rearden why he robs government relief ships. Ragnar's purpose is to restore to the producers the wealth stolen from them by the looters. (4) This is Dagny thinking to herself as she is about to run the first train on the John Galt Line. She realizes that a crowd of enthusiastic onlookers has gathered because an accomplishment of such magnitude is inspiring. (5) Eddie Willers says this to James Taggart. Eddie, who faces facts, drives home to Taggart the actual state of affairs on the Rio Norte Line. (6) This is Francisco speaking to Dagny. (Hugh Akston makes the same point to her.) This quote expresses the author's viewpoint that reality is intelligible to a rational being. Francisco can't be both a high-minded man of noble character and a worthless bum. If Dagny thinks he is both, she has made an error in reasoning and needs to examine her assumptions.

Discussion Questions

1. Why do the men of the mind go on strike?

2. What are the reasons for Rearden's willingness to support the family that seeks to destroy him?

3. Why does a great mind like Robert Stadler's believe that joining the looters is necessary?

4. In a book whose main positive characters are geniuses, what is the significance of a "common man" such as Eddie Willers?

5. Explain the "sanction of the victim" principle that Hank Rearden identifies and uses at his trial.

6. What are the causes of the Taggart Tunnel disaster?

Practice Projects

1. Stage a meeting between John Galt and the President of the United States. What would Galt say to him? How would the President respond? Create and enact a dialogue between the two. Perform the same activity with John Galt (or one of the novel's other main characters) and a different world leader.

2. Design a Web site to introduce *Atlas Shrugged* to other readers. What will you say to interest them in the book's story and ideas? Invite readers to post their thoughts regarding the novel.

3. Stage the following debates:

   a. A debate with Galt and the strikers on one side and Dagny and the scabs on the other, regarding the best way to defend the freedom of the mind in a country that's moving toward dictatorship.

   b. A debate between advocates of socialism and admirers of capitalism regarding the most moral and practical political/economic system.

4. Discuss—don't debate—what human society would be like if Galt's philosophy was dominant. What if the beliefs of Hank Rearden, as portrayed early in the story, were dominant? What if the looters' ideas were dominant? Whose ideas, if any from among the book's characters, are most influential in the world today? What are the practical consequences of these ideas?

5. Hold a simulated Constitutional Convention in which you revise some parts of the United States Constitution (as Judge Narragansett does near the end of the book) in accordance with the principles of John Galt.

6. Write a newspaper editorial defending Galt's principle of individual rights in opposition to the government's latest violation of those rights.

CliffsNotes Resource Center

The learning doesn't need to stop here. CliffsNotes Resource Center shows you the best of the best—links to the best information in print and online about Ayn Rand and works written by and about her. And don't think that this is all we've prepared for you; we've put all kinds of pertinent information at www.cliffsnotes.com. Look for all the terrific resources at your favorite bookstore or local library and on the Internet. When you're online, make your first stop www.cliffsnotes.com, where you'll find more useful information about *Atlas Shrugged*.

Books

If you're looking for more information about Ayn Rand and her other works, check out these publications.

Critical Works about Rand

Letters of Ayn Rand, edited by Michael Berliner, provides a collection of Ayn Rand's letters on topics ranging from Objectivism to advice for beginning writers. Includes an introduction by Leonard Peikoff. New York: Plume, 1997.

The Ayn Rand Lexicon: Objectivism from A to Z, edited by Harry Binswanger, offers an alphabetically arranged collection of Rand's writings on her philosophy of Objectivism. New York: New American Library Trade, 1990.

The Journals of Ayn Rand, edited by David Harriman, provides a personal look at Ayn Rand in her own words. Includes Rand's notes for her writing, essays, and thoughts on Hollywood and communism. New York: Plume, 1997.

The Ayn Rand Reader, edited by Gary Hull, contains excerpts from all of Rand's novels. Introduces readers to Rand's writing and philosophy. New York: Plume, 1999.

Objectivism: The Philosophy of Ayn Rand, by Leonard Peikoff, offers a renowned Ayn Rand scholar's explanation of Rand's philosophy. An excellent resource on Rand and Objectivism. New York: Meridian Books, 1993.

The Ominous Parallels, by Leonard Peikoff, explores the causes of Nazism and the parallels between the thoughts and beliefs in Nazi Germany and the United States. New York: Plume, 1997.

Rand's Major Works of Fiction

Anthem. 1961. New York: Plume, 1999.

Atlas Shrugged. 1957. New York: Signet, 1996.

The Fountainhead. 1943. New York: Signet, 1996.

We the Living. 1936. New York: New American Library, 1996.

The Early Ayn Rand: A Selection from Her Unpublished Fiction. New York: New American Library, 1986.

Rand's Major Works of Nonfiction

Capitalism: The Unknown Ideal. 1967. New York: New American Library, 1984.

For the New Intellectual. 1961. New York: New American Library, 1984.

Introduction to Objectivist Epistemology. Harry Binswanger and Leonard Peikoff, eds. New York: Meridian Books, 1990.

Philosophy: Who Needs It. 1982. New York: New American Library, 1985.

Return of the Primitive: The Anti-Industrial Revolution. Peter Schwartz, ed. New York: Meridian Books, 1999.

The Romantic Manifesto. 1971. New York: New American Library, 1975.

Russian Writings on Hollywood. Michael Berliner, ed. Marina del Ray, California: The Ayn Rand Institute Press, 1999.

The Virtue of Selfishness: A New Concept of Egoism. 1964. New York: New American Library, 1989.

The Voice of Reason: Essays in Objectivist Thought. New York: Meridian Books, 1990.

Internet

Check out these Web resources for more information about Ayn Rand or *Atlas Shrugged:*

The Ayn Rand Institute, aynrand.org—The Ayn Rand Institute Web site is an outstanding source of information regarding Rand's life, her books, her philosophy, and applications of Objectivism to current events and issues.

Journals of Ayn Rand, www.capitalism.org/journals/index .html—The unofficial Web site for the *Journals of Ayn Rand* offers excerpts from the book as well as comments from scholars and readers.

Second Renaissance Books, www.RationalMind.com @md This internet and catalogue marketer features the most complete selection of Ayn Rand's writings and recorded lectures available anywhere. For a free print catalogue, call 1-888-729-6149.

Next time you're on the Internet, don't forget to drop by www.cliffs-notes.com. We created an online Resource Center that you can use today, tomorrow, and beyond.

Films and Audio Recordings

Check out these films and audio recordings for more information on Ayn Rand:

Ayn Rand: A Sense of Life. Dir. Michael Paxton. Perf. Sharon Gless (narrator), Janne Peters, and Peter Sands. AG Media Corporation, Ltd. and Copasetic, Inc., 1997. A documentary film based on Ayn Rand's life.

Love Letters. Dir. William Dieterle. Perf. Jennifer Jones and Joseph Cotton. Paramount Pictures, 1945. A feature film written by Ayn Rand.

You can find these films and recordings for sale on the Internet or for rent at most local libraries and video stores.

Send Us Your Favorite Tips

In your quest for learning, have you ever experienced that sublime moment when you figure out a trick that saves time or trouble? Perhaps you realized that you were taking ten steps to accomplish something that could've taken two. Or, you found a little-known workaround that gets great results. If you've discovered a useful tip that helped you study more effectively and you'd like to share it, the CliffsNotes staff would love to hear from you. Go to our Web site at www.cliffsnotes.com and click the Talk to Us button. If we select your tip, we may publish it as part of CliffsNotes Daily, our exciting, free e-mail newsletter. To find out more or to subscribe to our newsletter, go to www.cliffsnotes.com on the Web.

Index

Check Out the All-New CliffsNotes Guides

TECHNOLOGY TOPICS

Balancing Your Checkbook with Quicken
Buying and Selling on eBay
Buying Your First PC
Creating a Winning PowerPoint 2000 Presentation
Creating Web Pages with HTML
Creating Your First Web Page
Exploring the World with Yahoo!
Getting on the Internet
Going Online with AOL
Making Windows 98 Work for You

Setting Up a Windows 98 Home Network
Shopping Online Safely
Upgrading and Repairing Your PC
Using Your First iMac
Using Your First PC
Writing Your First Computer Program

PERSONAL FINANCE TOPICS

Budgeting & Saving Your Money
Getting a Loan
Getting Out of Debt
Investing for the First Time
Investing in 401(k) Plans
Investing in IRAs
Investing in Mutual Funds
Investing in the Stock Market
Managing Your Money
Planning Your Retirement
Understanding Health Insurance
Understanding Life Insurance

CAREER TOPICS

Delivering a Winning Job Interview
Finding a Job on the Web
Getting a Job
Writing a Great Resume